the Russell'
Hope you
some good & useful
ideas in here.
GB

iRules

iRules

WHAT EVERY TECH-HEALTHY FAMILY
NEEDS TO KNOW ABOUT SELFIES, SEXTING,
GAMING, AND GROWING UP

Janell Burley Hofmann

RODALE.

© 2014 by Janell Burley Hofmann

Rodale books may be purchased for business or promotional use or for special sales. For information, please write to: Special Markets Department, Rodale Inc., 733 Third Avenue, New York, NY 10017.

Printed in the United States of America
Rodale Inc. makes every effort to use acid-free ♾, recycled paper ♻.

Book design by Joanna Williams

Library of Congress Cataloging-in-Publication Data is on file with the publisher.
ISBN-13: 978–1–62336–352–9   paperback

Distributed to the trade by Macmillan

2   4   6   8   10   9   7   5   3   1   paperback

We inspire and enable people to improve their lives and the world around them.
rodalebooks.com

Gregory, Brendan, Ella, Lily, and Cassidy, so truly, I thank you.
This—all of this—is for you . . .

Contents

A Note to the Reader

My children were yelled at in the making of this book. I lose my patience often. I make ridiculous threats like "If you don't stop fighting, there will be no Halloween!" I once gave my kids a bag of chocolate chips and locked the door to my office so I could do an Australian radio interview. My commitment to this family is downright overwhelming, as I'm sure yours is too. But we've got to be willing to show up and do the work. When you read this book, I am inviting you to grow, learn, and parent with me. This book is an intimate portrayal of the existence of technology in our lives and our homes, but also the beliefs, values, and stories that help shape our experiences with it. I share pieces of my life, the successes and the imperfections, as an offering. Take what you need. I am an expert only on what my family needs and what works within our home. I encourage you to do the same for your family. But I do believe the iRules model will bring balance, dialogue, and success to your family's relationship with technology.

Within these chapters, we will most definitely be exploring technology, its cultural impact, and the relationship our children have with it. But underneath that platform, we will be examining our truths, our stories, our lives. We cannot talk about parenting without calling up our core family values and beliefs. I invite you to fully join the conversation. As you continue through these pages, you will be given instructions on how to make your own family iRules. A collection of iRules makes a living, breathing agreement for behavior related to technology—one that suits your home, your parenting style, and your needs. iRules will allow you and your family to build healthy relationships with the technology used inside and outside your home.

We are more powerful together.

Janell

The Contract

Dear Gregory,

Merry Christmas! You are now the proud owner of an iPhone. Hot damn! You are a good and responsible thirteen-year-old boy and you deserve this gift. But with the acceptance of this present come rules and regulations. Please read through the following contract. I hope that you understand it is my job to raise you into a well-rounded, healthy young man that can function in the world and coexist with technology, not be ruled by it. Failure to comply with the following list will result in termination of your iPhone ownership.

I love you madly and look forward to sharing several million text messages with you in the days to come.

1. It is my phone. I bought it. I pay for it. I am loaning it to you. Aren't I the greatest?

2. I will always know the password.

3. If it rings, answer it. It is a phone. Say hello, use your manners. Do not ever ignore a phone call if the screen reads "Mom" or "Dad." Not ever.

4. Hand the phone to one of your parents promptly at 7:30 p.m. every school night and every weekend night at 9:00 p.m. It will be shut off for the night and turned on again at 7:30 a.m. If you would not make a call to someone's landline because their parents might answer first, then do not call or text. Listen to those instincts and respect other families like we would like to be respected.

5. It does not go to school with you. Have a conversation with the people you text. It's a life skill. Half days, field trips, and after-school activities will require special consideration.

6. If it falls into the toilet, smashes on the ground, or vanishes into thin air, you are responsible for the replacement cost or repairs. Mow a lawn, babysit, stash some birthday money. It will happen, you should be prepared.

7. Do not use this technology to lie to, fool, or deceive another human being. Do not involve yourself in conversations that are hurtful to others. Be a good friend first or stay the hell out of the crossfire.

8. Do not text, e-mail, or say anything through this device that you would not say in person.

9. Do not text, e-mail, or say anything to someone that you would not say out loud with their parents in the room. Censor yourself.

10. No porn. Search the Web for information you would openly share with me. If you have a question about anything, ask a person—preferably me or your father.

11. Turn it off, silence it, put it away in public. Especially in a restaurant, at the movies, or while speaking with another human being. You are not a rude person; do not allow the iPhone to change that.

12. Do not send or receive pictures of your private parts or anyone else's private parts. Don't laugh. Someday you will be tempted to do this despite your high intelligence. It is risky and could ruin your teenage, college, and/or adult life. It is always a bad idea. Cyberspace is vast and more powerful than you. And it is hard to make anything of this magnitude disappear—including a bad reputation.

13. Don't take a zillion pictures and videos. There is no need to document everything. Live your experiences. They will be stored in your memory for eternity.

14. Leave your phone home sometimes and feel safe and secure in that decision. It is not alive or an extension of you. Learn to live without it. Be bigger and more powerful than FOMO (fear of missing out).

15. Download music that is new or classic or different from what millions of your peers are listening to. Your generation has access to music like never before in history. Take advantage of that gift. Expand your horizons.

16. Play a game with words or puzzles or brainteasers every now and then.

17. Keep your eyes up. See the world happening around you. Stare out a window. Listen to the birds. Take a walk. Talk to a stranger. Wonder without googling.

18. You will mess up. I will take away your phone. We will sit down and talk about it. We will start over again. You and I, we are always learning. I am on your team. We are in this together.

It is my hope that you can agree to these terms. Most of the lessons listed here do not apply just to the iPhone, but to life. You are growing up in a fast and ever-changing world. It is exciting and enticing. Keep it simple every chance you get. Trust your powerful mind and giant heart above any machine. I love you. I hope you enjoy your awesome new iPhone.

xoxoxo,
Mom

Introduction

My oldest son, Gregory, just thirteen, had been asking for a cell phone for years. I had been adamant—preachy even—about children not needing such a device. Both my husband and I work in the town we live in and there are many people in our community web who would treat this boy like their own if he needed something. I saw it as a toy—a crutch, really—rather than a safety net as he was building some independence. Over and over again, I watched his young buddies leave their phones behind, lost between the couch cushions or tossed on the grass by the basketball hoop when they gathered for a game. They were just kids, often distracted by the temptation the phone offered, and I had struggled to assess the real value of ownership. It seemed like a burden. I didn't want the responsibility, the cost, or the trouble that seemed to come with it. Delaying it seemed like the only solution.

At some point, my boy had stopped asking and learned to navigate movie theaters and ice cream shops, our neighborhood and the town village without one. I had felt proud of this, borderline counter-cultural in my no-cell-phone philosophy. And with this lack of pressure over the past year or so, coupled with a general dip in his level of interest, I began to pay closer attention. He could text from his iPod, he could chat on the Xbox, and he could privately converse over the computer. The only thing he wasn't doing was talking on the phone, and that seemed like the most harmless (or at least the most familiar) risk of all. And naturally, when years twelve and thirteen rolled around, I saw that even though he didn't have one himself, the increased cell phone ownership among his peers expanded his exposure and upped his usage anyway. I would constantly find him head down, chatting and texting on cell phones belonging to others. See, I had convinced myself that I was protecting my boy from the technology, but we had long ago been invaded.

I had to reevaluate my position and get off my soapbox. In doing so, my stubbornness softened. I saw my flawed perspective. Not allowing him to own the technology didn't stop him from using it. It did, however, stop me from teaching him how to use it. Therein lies a colossal difference. Mixed with some giant strides in his degree of maturity, teaching him became the ultimate motivator for the inevitable next step—getting him his own cell phone. Suddenly it felt crucial to grant him access to this world of technology with his parents as his guides.

• • •

About a month before Christmas, our cell phone plan notifies us it is offering an older-model iPhone at a very low purchase price. I am hesitant. I do not know if this is the right place to begin the cell phone journey. But my husband and I have iPhones and my boy, the music-loving, picture-sharing, video-creating social butterfly, would love a seat on our family iCloud. We might not get this deal again, especially at a time when we can handle the data plan fees and still wow a boy who just doesn't see this gift coming.

As the days lead to Christmas, I lie awake at night hoping he's ready to handle this access to the entire world, with unimaginable privacy, at a time in his adolescent development where risk is the reward. I think of the ways I have prepared for this moment without ever knowing it. In my everyday life, I write and lead parenting workshops and wellness programs for families. Over the years, I've talked to older children's parents that I like and respect to see what obstacles they've encountered and what their limits and boundaries are on technology, and to laugh with them at and learn from their funny mishaps. I've read articles, books, and other resources about the parental settings offered on devices. I've set up meetings with the county's youth sheriff officer about Internet safety for some of the teens and families with whom I work. I began to notice that at almost every parenting workshop or family program I led, the discussion would eventually circle around to technology. I maintain a living conversation and pulse through my community connections, and it was clear we were all looking to establish some boundaries for and guidelines on the increasing use of electronic devices by our children. And I have always brought these outside discussions into our home to keep us informed and engaged.

Hope that I've had enough open and honest conversations with Gregory about choices. I hope he remembers the stories I have shown him about real-life actions and consequences—the teenage girl who blogged about having shared a topless photo that was ruining her reputation even years later, the effects on growing adolescents of the chronic sleep disruption caused by devices at the bedside, and the celebrity who tweeted something in haste and then regretted it. I hope he knows that while I give him this gift with trust, as an offering of my love and respect for him, I will always be the person he can come to if he finds himself mixed up in the trouble and chaos it can bring. Does he know all this? I decide to comb through all these pieces collected in my mind and take note.

And then I wrap his gift and wait with anticipation as it sits under the tree, hidden in a giant box to trick him. On Christmas morning, he tears it open, searches through the endless paper for the small and powerful gift buried in the corner of the box. He smiles, his authentic boyhood smile, while bouncing a little and says, "Is this real?!" We laugh and hug; he is genuine in his gratitude. Within minutes he is charging it, arranging and customizing his apps. He collects the phone numbers of his peers and extended family and sends a giant blast with a picture of himself on his new scooter, wearing oversized slippers and plaid pj's, that reads "Merry Christmas! I got an iPhone! This is my new number!" We are all trapped in this group text—grandparents, faraway uncles, family friends, and dozens of thirteen-year-olds, wishing each other merry, happy, joy, and bragging about a wide variety of gifts and school vacation plans until the wee hours of Christmas night. The adults beg the teens to start a new conversation without us. My son is embarrassed that he has included everyone in a group conversation that lasts through several hundred texts. I am reminded of the importance of teaching and guiding him, that he's still learning too. As I tuck him into bed on the twenty-fifth, we agree to meet and discuss some house rules for the iPhone the following morning. Late that night, my collection of mental and physical notes, my love for this child, and the reality of iPhone ownership swirl together with ease and the iPhone contract is born.

I ask my husband to review the contract. We discuss it, he polishes some points. Though he is often baffled by my openness and honesty with our kids, I can tell he appreciates the way the contract's bullet points cut right to it. He thinks it is fair, that nothing should be a surprise to our son. He thinks it's funny and good-natured, and casually mentions how it really applies to life in general.

I ask my son to read it. He smiles wide and says, "Hey, Mom, you're really good at this. I don't think you left anything out." He makes a change to the point about never bringing it to school—we agree he can bring it to school when field trips are scheduled and on days when he has after-school sports. We edit and reprint. Overall, he's not affected. He says he feels like he would naturally follow those rules— he likes his sleep uninterrupted, hates social drama, has no issue with my knowing the passwords as long as I'm not a "creeper." We all move on pretty quickly, but I feel so much better for having set these expectations and boundaries. I feel like I have done my job as a parent.

Much of what I teach in my workshops is implicit in the rules of the contract, so I share it with clients, friends, and family, including my editor, Farah Miller, at the *Huffington Post*. She adds it to my blog page on the site and sends me a gentle reply e-mail that reads, "This is genuine and sincere. There is nothing cliché about it. Parents are thirsty for this kind of material. Get ready and hold on." Less than an hour later, Arianna Huffington tweets it. The following morning, less than twenty-four hours after it posted, the crew of *Good Morning America* is in my kitchen for an interview. The contract is deemed the "first viral sensation of 2013," and for months, media requests and opportunities pour in. Overflowing with attention, my inbox flooded with feedback, my son looks at me days later as we're up to our eyeballs in interviews and conversations and says, "No offense, Mom, but what's the big deal? Don't all parents do this?"

I guess not. With almost all teens going online, many children as young as six owning cell phones, and tweens entering the social networking system, many parents don't know where to begin. According to a paper published in the medical journal *Pediatrics,* children and teens spend more time using various media than they do on any other activity except sleeping. Families are understandably exhausted by the responsibilities of parenting, and tackling technology can feel overwhelming. Where do we begin? How do we enforce boundaries in partnership with our children? We need clarity and an understanding of this ever-changing technology. As you know, smartphones are only the beginning. Whether it's iPads, Xboxes, laptops, apps, Twitter, Instagram, Facebook, Snapchat, FaceTime, Skype, or texting, there is so much to learn and navigate within our homes. According to *Always Connected,* a report from the Joan Ganz Cooney Center at Sesame Workshop, children ages eight to eighteen are exposed to all media, including television, computer and video games, and MP3 players, for ten hours and forty-five minutes every day. Current devices allow multiple activities (like Web surfing, online chatting, TV watching, and music playing) to happen simultaneously. How do we manage all of this?

The stories I hear every day are not in the headlines. They are not about the horrific and tragic cyberbullied-teen suicides, identity theft victims, or online pedophiles. They are the stories that individually will never be picked up by the press but are changing the way we live, how we behave and interact with one another. The subjects of these stories include a high school English teacher whose students took a video of her when she bent to pick up a marker and shared it online; a group of teenage girls who shared pictures of each other sleeping or changing in the locker room on social networking sites without permission; the parent who was worried about the violent video games being played at the home of her son's friend when he visited; the four-year-old who went to visit cousins and was allowed to play with the iPad for hours. These stories, these conversations and questions about behavior, inter-action, and etiquette are bubbling to the surface in homes every-where. Every day I hear from parents desperate for guidance and dialogue on how to deal with these scenarios. Parents are eager for strategies and tools they can use to navigate the new norm of porta-ble, accessible technology making its way into every moment and every avenue of our lives.

Since the initial iPhone contract was created, I have expanded it to include all types of technology in the home under an umbrella agree-ment that I call the iRules. In my workshops, speaking appearances, and coaching sessions, I advocate that each family have its own iRules contract establishing guidelines for technology use. The iRules con-tract is now used as a model by parents and families creating their own iRules. I have had hundreds of requests for copies of the contract, and I field questions every day from parents, schools, and church and par-ent groups desperate for a road map for developing their own iRules or starting their own conversations on technology use.

Whether it's during my weekly tech etiquette spot on American Public Media's *Marketplace Tech* on NPR, in a workshop, or in a coach-ing session, most parents I talk to ask for the same palpable thing—

ideas to help them nurture human connections and develop and model using technology with respect and integrity. This mission is what I call Slow Tech Parenting (there's more about this below). The answer to the question of how to execute this in a practical way is different for each family, perhaps even different for every child, but the methods for developing the iRules are the same. Each family has to establish its own living and breathing contract on acceptable behavior for technology—one that suits the home, the parenting style, the children's ages, and the types of technology. In this book, I will relate my family's technology experiences, as well as those of other families, educators, community members, and professionals who work with children and families. The information and strategies presented in this book will help you preserve your personal connections while still enjoying all the benefits of technology. I'll also share data and tools that will help you engage with and educate yourself on the technology so you'll no longer feel overwhelmed by it.

iRules will adapt the principles of my contract for your children based on your own family's values and philosophies. This book is a manifesto on parenting in a technological age. The best way to deal with the present and future challenges is to return to the parenting basics. The pitfall many parents succumb to is the belief that the rules have somehow changed, just because technology has. But that isn't the case. Instead, *we just need to apply the same parenting strategies and beliefs to the technology!* Parents must identify and outline the principles and values that underlie their parenting cornerstones and then adapt and apply those to the technology. Then you'll have your own set of iRules that reflect the parenting philosophies currently in use in your home.

As a guide, I will share my three parenting cornerstones: respect, responsibility, and encouragement to live fully. Separate sections will explore the practical application of each of these cornerstones to technology use.

Our children's lives are no longer limited to school, home, and the playground. They are fully immersed in a new online world that has its own etiquette, language, and potential problems. This book will shed light on the broad, varied, and ever-changing ways children and teens participate online, exposing how we can help our children not only survive but also thrive with technology. Our ability to guide them in a technological age has great implications for their attention span, self-confidence, self-image, and social world.

Children who feel emotionally and physically cared for, guided, and attended to have higher self-esteem. They make better choices online and respect rules. When children see they are valued by being given secure boundaries and respect, a bond of trust is built between parent and child. The most powerful message in this book is that the technology may change, but the teaching of self-respect, integrity, and responsibility does not.

When I began writing this book, I started really digging within myself. I had to look at my parenting philosophies and my motivations for wanting to bring this book and these ideas to life for other families. I couldn't share anything with you until I was certain I fully understood myself and the message I wanted to convey. And then, in a discussion with my gifted agent, Amy Hughes, we started talking about how important it is for us to coexist with technology, live in balance, use it with purpose. And there it was! Just like the slow food movement and the slow living movement, we have our very own Slow Tech Parenting movement! Slow Tech Parents are finding a balance between technology and human interaction by engaging in a form of active parenting that integrates traditional interpersonal relationships with technology by using text messaging, picture and info sharing, video calling, and social networking as opportunities to enhance the balanced life. The tech savvy, the tech weary, and generation tech can come together under the Slow Tech umbrella to bridge the gap between technology and living with purpose.

Meet the Family

The Hofmann Family

The Parents

Adam: Age 37

Roles: Superhero, father of five children

Tech Bio: Technology MVP. Can fix, assemble, and troubleshoot any computer, television, or electronic device. Designs Web sites for fun and with ease despite having no formal training. Addicted to researching and purchasing high-tech gadgets. Loves Apple products' intuitiveness and expansive access to music on services like Spotify. Quit social networking sites a year ago for no reason and doesn't miss a minute of it.

Janell: Age 34

Roles: Public speaker, writer, mother of five children

Tech Bio: Family's most-improved tech genius, or texpert (self-appointed). Uses Facebook, Twitter, and Instagram daily. Breaks out in anxiety hives when on Pinterest, but can't stop looking at it. iPhone's number one fan. Addicted to picture taking and changing filters and borders to make photos look artsy. Blogger. E-reader. Streamer. Mile tracker. Podcast and music listener.

The Offspring

Gregory: Age 14

Role: Junior high school student

Tech Bio: Proud owner of an iPhone (with accompanying contract!). Loves texting and Xbox 360. Has personal e-mail,

Xbox, Twitter, Instagram, Skype, Snapchat, YouTube, Vine, and Kik accounts.

Brendan: Age 11

Role: Fifth-grader

Tech Bio: Loves Xbox 360. Would sell his soul for five extra minutes of *Minecraft* or *Clash of Clans* on the iPad. Has very limited access to Gregory's old iPod Touch (but no social networking accounts), which is used mainly for music. Has a Nintendo DS that sits in the closet. Has recently started begging for an Instagram account.

Ella: Age 9

Role: Fourth-grader

Tech Bio: Loves the iPad for watching YouTube music videos and searching Google for pictures of and ads for puppies and horses. Delighted by apps like Angry Birds and Cut the Rope. Streams TV shows I haven't approved and watches them quietly under a blanket.

Lily: Age 7

Role: Second-grader

Tech Bio: Fights for time on the family iPad for playing games, using apps, and doing Math Fact practice. Loves *Minecraft*. Has an iPod for music, likes to sneak tiny games on it.

Cassidy: Age 5

Role: Kindergartner

Tech Bio: Owns a secondhand iPod that is usually lost or not charged, which makes her cry, but so does not owning one, so there's no winning. Has a genuine iPad addiction.

And We're Off!

As if parenting books weren't exhausting enough, you've decided to pick up a *parenting technology* book. The vastness, the learning curve, the horror! I promise it doesn't have to hurt! Take it one step at a time. First, ask yourself the questions on page xxv. Assess yourself. And know that you are not alone in being tempted to turn a blind eye because it all seems overwhelming. Even if you are a technology professional—or a tech mastermind—parenting with this stuff is new to all of us. Even if you have an itty-bitty baby and think you have at least a decade to rest before the raging hormones and bad choices are knocking at the door (or tweeting to the phone), know that the technology creeps in—you'll become familiar with plugged-in preschool playdates, video game ratings, and social networking accounts for second-graders. Even if your babies are already in high school, your tech wisdom can and will help them navigate the freedom of young adulthood, the professional world, and beyond. Because yes, in this book we will be talking tech nitty-gritty—the how-to details, the nagging questions, sharing stories and circumstances. But we'll also be talking about family values like respect and responsibility and priorities like living fully and mindfully. The way you parent the technology will not be far removed from how you parent in the everyday. And that's the point!

Ready, Set . . . Wait!

I could be all wrong. I had a father write to me and say in part, "You've got it all wrong. What you care about doesn't matter. So what if our kids stare at screens or only communicate virtually? You are overthinking this. Everything you are trying to hold on to will be obsolete to our children. This is the future. Let it go."

I thought about this critically. I really did. I have been known to care, process, discuss, and dissect intensively (this will become very clear to you in the pages ahead). And in some ways I agree. Technology is the future. Our children will know only a world with it. Why dwell on it? And in some ways I disagree. We have a unique perspective on this massive cultural shift because we have known the world both with and without widespread technology. We can choose to preserve pieces. We can protect childhood and foster experiences—real ones. I don't know why staring out the window during a car trip instead of staring down at a phone means so damn much to me—but it does! And I don't fully understand why teaching our children to look up into the eyes of the person who takes our ice cream cone order or putting our phones away when we have dinner with a friend feels so much more important to me than almost any other cause right now. But I think that if we vow not to lose these tiny, critical connections and instead use the technology with purpose, then perhaps we really will be unstoppable. We can change and create all things. I mean this.

So I may be all wrong. I may be wildly overthinking this stuff. But all of these words and thoughts, I need to get them out. I need to share them. Because here's the thing—I've never felt more right.

Quiz It!

Do you answer any of these questions with a "Yes!"?

- Have you ever felt overwhelmed by the number of social networking sites available to your child? Do you know how to use them yourself?
- Are you worried that insisting that your children tell you their passwords and give you a current list of their online accounts will make them believe you don't trust them?
- Do you know who your kids are talking to and playing with online?
- Are you engaged in power struggles with your young children over portable devices and screen time?
- Are you unsure how to navigate privacy settings and parental controls?
- Are you guilty of chronic technology use and worried about the behavior you're modeling for your children?
- Are your kids and teens always head down over their devices or glued to their gaming more than you'd like?
- Have you witnessed or are you worried about inappropriate online behavior and unsure of how to talk about it with your child?
- Do you resent technology? Does learning and parenting technology seem daunting?
- Have you noticed a cultural shift in manners, social interactions, and mindfulness?
- Do you want to preserve childhood away from the screen?
- Do you want to embrace and teach your children to use modern technology without being ruled by it?
- Are you doing nothing at all to address your child's use of technology? Is it time to do more?

Results: If you feel like closing this book because these questions make you feel guilty, overwhelmed, or annoyed—wait, I understand! We've all been there, but we can do this together. If you feel like you are already parenting technology perfectly—wait! I have a lot to say. Take what you can use and leave the rest. I promise you'll learn something new, or at least find something that will ignite discussion.

PART 1

Respect

Be kind to others, tell the truth, use your voice for good, create positive relationships, eat well, sleep well, love yourself, be brave, lead.

● ○ ○

Awareness and Action

iRule: Talk! And Talk Some More!

> **My iRule:** It is my phone. I bought it. I pay for it.
> I am loaning it to you. Aren't I the greatest?

When we became parents, we did not know this would be our fate. We did not know that the technology would burst into our lives with such intensity and appeal. We did not know that every one of us—including our children—would be engaged in a different and equally powerful way. Well, at least I didn't know. When I first became a mother in 1999, I was still finishing my bachelor's degree. We had a desktop computer and I used it for one sole purpose—word processing. I was a picture of focus as I finished papers and projects during newborn naps and in the wee hours of the night. Of course I had e-mail too. But it seemed secondary to calling someone on the phone or meeting for coffee and doughnuts. I remember when Gregory was about eighteen months old, we had cable Internet installed in the tiny corner room of our apartment. *This was living.* It was so fast. I could research and shop and listen and browse without being at a computer lab or using dial-up or waiting. I was in awe of the potential this one computer had and all the ways I could access the world—in an instant—from my humble home.

Just as Gregory's language skills started to develop, so did his interest in the computer. He'd wake up in the morning all warm and sleepy, and as I picked that sturdy baby body up into my arms, he'd say, "Elmo! 'Puter!" How sweet. I thought he was so smart. I mean, I'd never met a computer-loving baby. It was endearing, really. We would have breakfast and then sit down together at the "'puter" and play. He would be on my lap asking for "Sesame-dot-com" or "Bob the Builder." At first he would point and I would click and we'd play together, snuggled up and squealing over our favorite characters. But over time, he'd push my hand right out of the way and navigate the mouse himself. He wanted to sit alone: "No, Mom, I do it." He became obsessed with the games and stories and songs all at his fingertips, animated and exciting. The fun was predictable enough to delight, but a two-year-old could control or alter just enough of the action to make it worth coming back for more. He'd see computers in the homes of his grandparents and friends and beg for a turn. We had to start setting timers, distracting him, using tools to redirect his attention, and shutting down the computer completely for hours so use was nonnegotiable. I'm laughing now, as I dig through my memory for our tech beginnings, thinking that we have been creating and negotiating iRules for most of Greg's life.

But even then, though I saw how drawn to and immersed in the computer he was, I don't think I fully understood what was unfolding. Even if I had been told that someday very soon, Gregory could have that computer inside a small cell phone, with an added camera and various easy communication tools, and bring it anywhere he wanted in his back pocket, I would have never believed you. *No person will ever need that, never mind a child,* I would have thought. But here we are. We are the generation of parents who are the bridge between "before" and "after" the technology. We lived our own childhoods without and we are raising the first generation with. We have the benefit of insight and wisdom gleaned from our tech-free past. But we have no one ahead of us leading the way to our tech future. So what can we do right now? How can we parent the technology in the present with the knowledge, tools, and instincts we have in this very moment in time?

I believe dialogue to be the most critical piece in raising children. Through parent-and-child conversation, we can solve, discuss, prevent, laugh, connect, disagree, understand, share, and grow. We need to start talking. We need to ask questions. We need to share stories. We need to talk to our partners and extended family members. We need to start conversations in the community with educators, pediatricians, neighbors. We need to assess our family's wants, needs, goals, and values in general and then apply them to the technology—even if our results look very different from someone else's. Because when we talk to our children, to our families, and within our communities, we do not feel alone. We share our perspectives and gather strength from both shared and opposing viewpoints. We start to feel secure in our views and we become stronger parents because of it.

When we feel overwhelmed as parents, we need to hold ourselves up. And high! We cannot back down from the knowledge that *we are the parents.* We are the authority. Not controlling, overbearing, no-freedom-to-make-a-mistake parents, but our children's models and lifelong guides. We can lovingly walk the path with them while enforcing boundaries and limits. Families must be proud of their choices and get in touch with their truth about raising a family. But parenting is part natural and part learned. We need to take our parenting seriously and to regard it as one of the greatest responsibilities we will ever have, which means making a commitment to trust our core parental instincts and seek out resources and services available to help us grow.

iRules may look different for each of us. For example, parents that don't pick their kids up from school until 7:00 p.m. may allow their children later tech hours than I do, because Greg gets home most days at 2:45. We all have different daily routines and needs, but we can use the same strategies to build our own sets of boundaries in our own homes. Before we begin with our first step, a Tech Talk, we must have specific conversations and assess a series of our own feelings and beliefs.

Before Your Tech Talk

You must come together! A key component of making your iRules a success is to have complete accord with your spouse, partner, or anyone parenting with you. This may mean scheduling discussions without the children present, ironing out varied views or opinions to maintain a united front, and allowing all of those involved in raising your children to contribute to the creation of your family iRules. This is crucial and cannot be avoided. Teamwork makes the dream work!

Although I composed our family iRules, Adam and I had been having discussions about our tech beliefs for years. He is a tech lover in some ways—he appreciates devices' functionality, purposes, streamlining—while I'm a tech lover in others—I value and use devices socially, for picture taking, texting, sharing. Both sets of interests impacted our iRules contract. As we watched the technology evolve and make its way to younger and younger children, we talked. We talked about articles we'd read and conversations we'd had with other people. Before I showed Greg our iRules contract, Adam looked at it, made changes and additions to make sure that we could both agree to parent it consistently.

As you begin these discussions about technology, ask yourself, how does the technology feel? Assess your own feelings and values about specific technologies. Do you feel confident in knowing how the technology works or are you intimidated? How do you feel when your children use that technology? When your daughter is staring down at the smartphone screen for hours, do you want to scream? If you see your son playing violent video games, do you cringe? When your toddler collapses on the floor crying for the iPad, do you feel helpless? Note these feelings so you can address specific boundaries head-on while being aware of your emotional temperature in each instance.

I have to admit that I can be tense around technology. I studied mass media in college, and the impacts that papers, projects, discussions, lectures, and my thesis research had have never left me. I saw how media use influences perception and behavior—especially media used without mindfulness—and how easily our views and opinions can be altered by the images and messages we see and process. I never wanted my sons or daughters to get their information or beliefs about gender roles from the media. I wanted to be the one to promote and encourage their personal reflections on who they are and who they want to be. So that remains a priority for me. You will find that your personal history and experiences will influence your tolerance for tech. As we start to learn more about ourselves and our parenting styles, we become much clearer on the deliberate direction we want to take with our children.

Certain types of television shows and video games make me squirm. I wish the kids would watch *Arthur* and play *Madden* forever because of their innocence. It's important to me that my children build positive relationships, and it's hard to see how thousands of young teens spending all day on social networking sites promotes that. But the more I dug into and prepared my own set of iRules and the values underlying that agreement, the more easily I could see that my influences were very present. My standards were clear, so I could let go and allow Greg to enjoy social networking within the boundaries of my parenting philosophies.

We need to understand our parenting motivations. We need to

know why we are inclined to react or relate, freak out or turn a blind eye. Knowing yourself will help you parent with the clearest convictions. When a parent is certain about who they are, what they stand for, and what they need and want for their children, the boundaries and styles come together with ease. Don't be afraid to dig below the surface, to get to know yourself. Does the technology in your home make you scared? What are you afraid of? Make a list! Online predators? Tech addiction? Lack of exercise? Loss of imagination? Once we name our biggest fears, we can start to devise specific rules and tools to help us deal with them so they don't become realities. When Greg got the iPhone, I was scared that he would become addicted to it, bring or sneak it everywhere. I already had a full and busy parenting life bubbling over with endless challenges that called on me to apply all of my greatest skills and tools every day to negotiate. I didn't want the iPhone to bring us past a breaking point. I wanted to be able to parent it with my full attention. And I knew that my greatest fear was that I would lose Greg to the iPhone—that this device would become his world and everything else would become less than it. So I made several iRules to help us both make sure that didn't happen without consequences.

And then we need to see each child as an individual. I say this like it's effortless. But I know it is not. I almost always lump my kids together by gender (and age): "The girls can't watch that show, please change it." Or "The boys are tired tonight, so they need to head up to bed early." The more children you have, the harder it can be to decipher and tend to individual needs. But with technology, I think it's important to create a kid profile. Think about each child. List their ages, interests, tendencies, personality traits, struggles, etc. This will help you brainstorm what needs to be in your iRules. Does your child like the outdoors or spend more time indoors? Is your child naturally sociable or shy? Is homework a challenge? Is the calendar filled with activities?

Here is a profile I created for Brendan when we made our iRules for his tech use.

> **Brendan:** Age eleven. Loves basketball and soccer, plays constant neighborhood pickup games with a large group of friends. Breezes through homework without help, self-directed. Needs ten hours of sleep but constantly pushes for a later bedtime, as well as extra snacks and different dinners, and fusses for more technology time. Wants to have the same tech limits as Greg, who's three grades older.

> **What I learned:** I'll need to be firm and leave no room for negotiation on tech use because he tends to push for more of everything. I do worry that he'll try to push the boundaries on games deemed inappropriate (especially when he's not at home). I'm not worried that he won't go outside, get exercise, or socialize. I'm not worried about him as a student. He's busy and active, so he needs to eat well and get to bed early. For Brendan, no screens (except family TV or computer homework) during the week works best.

These two small paragraphs are a great foundation for building iRules for Brendan. I can take information I have gathered about myself and the person/people with whom I am raising my family, our parenting philosophies, and my child's profile to begin creating working iRules. We can all set rules and consequences as parents. It's Parenting 101: "Your curfew is 9:00. If you come home at 9:01, you are grounded for a week." There are situations that call for this type of black-and-white, right-and-wrong parenting method. But technology can be a little trickier, because parts can be gray. We need to focus on creating a *working* set of boundaries, ones that breed success and limit struggle. This is why iRules work so well—they are adaptable to every child, family, situation, and scenario. You are setting your child up to have success with technology while being guided by the most trusted people in their lives—their parents. An iRules contract is a unique and powerful parenting tool that fosters success for both the individual and the entire family system.

Start with a Tech Talk

Now that you have identified your parenting beliefs and core values and profiled each of your children and their needs and behaviors, it's time to Tech Talk. The Tech Talk is a deliberate conversation you must have with each of your children regarding the specific technology they use. Tech Talks can happen in phases and be revisited at any time to make revisions, discuss a situation, or assess the use of newly introduced technology. The technology and the way it is used are constantly changing, as is the development of our children. Stay tuned in and be open to adapting your iRules during Tech Talks! Before having that talk, read this chapter over.

Ideally, a Tech Talk happens prior to the start of use—being proactive instead of reactive is best—but a lot of the time our kids are using new technology before we know it. That's why a tech inventory is the best place to start.

Tech Talk Phase 1: Info Gathering

- What technologies are you using?
- Can you explain the basics and teach me how to use the ones I'm not familiar with?
- Will you show me your online profile?
- When do you like to use the specific technology and why?

Tech Talk Phase 2: Define Expectations

- For each technology used, present your vision for ideal and appropriate use, including time limits, expectations, etc.
- Tech Talks can occur whenever and as often as you want them to.
- Be clear and direct, but open enough to ask and answer questions.

○   The length and depth of each conversation will vary depending on your child's age and temperament, the amount of technology in the home, and what was said in previous Tech Talks.

○   If you need to digest and consider the information you get before establishing ground rules, you can adjourn and return later with the specific limits and boundaries of your iRules.

Sample: Here is what I expect from you: You can play the Xbox on Fridays from after school through bedtime and on Sundays until 5:00 p.m. You can play games that are rated up to T for teen, but you must get parent approval before buying or playing anything new.

Tech Talk Phase 3: Meet Again!

○   Keep the Tech Talks alive! Don't wait until there is a crisis or a struggle going on. Schedule regular Tech Talks to keep the communication open.

○   For example, did your daughter get a new social networking account or a new iPad as she entered high school? Come together again for a Tech Talk.

○   Have you noticed a change in behavior? Perhaps your son is purchasing a series of video games without your approval and it's making you uncertain. Schedule another Tech Talk.

A "Meet Again" Tech Talk with Greg

Greg: Mom, can we sit down and talk about the iRules for the summer? I really think that 7:30 is too early on summer weeknights for me to turn off my phone.

Me: I totally agree. Let me just check in with Daddy and we'll come up with a plan.

A day or so later, we sit down briefly and agree that up to 9:00 on summer nights is acceptable for talking, texting, and FaceTime interactions. Because Greg has more freedom in the summer, I do understand that on some nights, he may scroll through social networking sites later than that. By 10:00, we're on complete shutdown. As it turns out, on most nights he's fast asleep by then.

You may encounter pushback. One of the thornier topics of discussion during our Tech Talks with Greg is the ratings and appropriateness of certain video games. I have established firm boundaries for general use, but I am more flexible* if his siblings are not home or are sleeping, the sound is turned off, the window of time to play is limited, and (dear God, I'm actually saying this) the blood setting is turned off. Yes! There is actually a setting on many video games that makes them less intense by not allowing blood to be seen during violent scenes.

---

*I realize that I do not sound flexible here. But I really hate most video games and I personally don't get their appeal, so instead of throwing them all into the Atlantic, this is my compromise: Play them by my guidelines or don't play them. Okay, totally not flexible at all, but you get the idea.

If you don't know how to use the technology your child is engaging with, take time after the talk to learn about it. You don't have to be proficient, but at least teach yourself the basics and know the sites where your kids are going online. Personally, whether I was parenting it or not, I would use Facebook, Twitter, and Instagram. I have no real need for a Vine or Snapchat account. But Gregory does use both, so I have an account with each because I wanted to fully understand how they work. Even though I hardly ever use either site, I feel like I have a more active understanding of their appeal and how they are used. This helps me have easier conversations about the sites with Gregory because I can reference and understand the lingo.

Don't be afraid to adjust your expectations based on what's working and what isn't working in your iRules. Your Tech Talks are the jumping-off points for your family guidelines, and they will grow, change, and evolve with you. Just keep Tech Talking!

Help!

When I do Tech Talk workshops for families or bump into someone at the post office or grocery store, one of the most common situations I hear about goes something like this: "Janell, I am so furious. You will never believe it—my son got a Twitter account without my permission. I didn't even know he was on Twitter! I specifically said that every account must be parent approved until he turns sixteen, but then he went and did it anyway! And for a month, he's been on it and I had no idea. I just don't know what to do."

I can sympathize with them about their child's relentless wanting. Brendan, who's currently in fifth grade, hounds me for iChat and Instagram accounts on Greg's old iPod Touch.*

---

*Wait, I'm not supposed to call it "Greg's old iPod Touch" anymore. Brendan prefers that I call it what it is: "Brendan's iPod Touch that I don't trust him with, because I treat him like a baby." And we're clear.

The boy hounds me. I tell him we're taking it slow, that in time he'll get to use all of the features, but for now let's just practice with the current settings and apps. On his best days he agrees to this and can see the big picture. On his worst days he tells me I just want the timing to be perfect so I can make him a contract like Greg's and go on TV and get famous again. He called my mother, Nan Sue, and asked her for her opinion on the matter: Didn't she think I was being overprotective? Kids. Either way, for now, I'm not budging. And my mom brilliantly agreed to stay out of it. At least that's what they told me.

But if Brendan did get an account without my knowing it, so help me, I don't know what I'd do. I can understand the parent's confusion, the feelings of betrayal and fury. But after the dust settled, the clarity would set in. It would look like this: Bye-bye, iPod Touch and any chance of us fulfilling Brendan's other tech desires. Unapproved account: deleted. Additional consequences: loss of some non-tech cherished privilege, like a basketball game or an afternoon with friends.

We're talking betraying our trust, lying, sneaking, and having a general disregard for parental boundaries. Someday when I felt like perhaps he had some increased understanding and maturity, we could revisit these consequences (without ever forgetting this teachable experience). This type of behavior makes my job as a parent very easy. But that's just me.

What I would actually say to this parent is "What are your consequences for other forms of betrayal, like sneaking to a friend's house, being disrespectful to a teacher, or lying about breaking something?" Treat it the same way. Don't be afraid to apply your usual parenting strategies to the technology. There needs to be a consequence, so even if you let the child keep the account, hold them accountable for their actions. And don't just leave it at giving out the punishment! Do not lose this opportunity to discuss the experience. Ask all those juicy parenting questions.

- Why did you set up an account when I said no?
- Why was the need so great that you needed to sneak?
- How are you using the technology?
- How can we be sure this doesn't happen again?
- Help me understand this situation better. Did you think I wouldn't find out?
- Did you think I wouldn't care?

A Great Bridge to Build: Say, "I'm not keeping the technology from you to hurt you. I'm learning it too, and I need to be certain we're all prepared to use these sites and accounts the best way we can."

House iRule!

As stated, it is best to meet with each child individually for a Tech Talk. But you may also have some house iRules that apply to everyone. In our house, we don't play with the iPad or Xbox during the school week. This was announced during a family Tech Talk over dinner when we were discussing ideas and behaviors relevant to the whole group. Because I have so many children in a close age range, there had been numerous sibling struggles over turns on the iPad and computer—especially between my girls. I was in a constant state of negotiation with them—setting the timer and keeping track of who played what and when, who did their chores so they could have twenty minutes to play, what YouTube videos were acceptable, who went first last time. With after-school activities, homework, family dinner, and non-tech playtime, there was simply no space for recreational tech use. So I just made it easy and ruled it out. Sometimes we just need to eliminate the struggle. And on Saturday mornings, when I'm out for a run or having my coffee with Adam on the porch, they can wrestle with and claw at each other over the iPad to their hearts' content.

The Wee Ones

A formal Tech Talk may not be necessary with very young kids. But having a modified one is great. Weave it into your life. You may already do this without realizing it. Your littlest ones may already know they can't bring technology to the dinner table or into their bedrooms at night. They may already know that after lunch is the time they can have a chance to play with the iPad or computer before their nap. Children love routine and rhythms, so iRules don't need to be forced and formal, they will evolve naturally based on the family schedule and needs. Little kids thrive with structure and they want to please their parents.

Sometimes they even enforce the rule themselves. My young nieces, ages one to four, would yell out to their mom, "No phone while you're driving, Mommy!" if she reached to answer it or respond to a text in the car. When I asked how the kids knew this rule, my brother-in-law and his wife said they had talked about driving and using cell phones not being a safe combination (and against the law where they live) and that they had agreed as a couple to break the habit of talking or texting while driving, even when stopped at a red light. Because the girls were around for and often part of these conversations, they caught on and understood the expectation. It's never too early to start talking about healthy behaviors, expectations, limits, and tech etiquette, even in modified forms. Just like we start talking about physical health, sexual health, and drug and alcohol use long before our children are at risk or going through puberty, we need to model and practice healthy tech behaviors in advance.

This tactic is not used to scare children and make them worry, it is about being comfortable talking and sharing with our children in an age-appropriate way. Often we need to tailor our conversations to make them appropriate for different ages. Here is an example of how I might talk to each of my children.

To Cassidy (five): "We only use the iPad a little bit and not all the time. It's important that we have enough time to play outside and go to the library and see our friends. That stuff keeps us healthy and happy. The iPad is really fun, but too much of it isn't good for our smart brains and strong bodies."

To Ella (nine): "I don't mind if you take the iPad into your room to listen to music, but I don't want you on Web sites or YouTube videos that I didn't approve. Sometimes we see pictures or videos online by mistake that we wish we didn't see or aren't good for us. Sometimes they're jokes or not real and sometimes they are, but it's hard to know the difference or understand why on earth people would post all sorts of weird and crazy stuff. I just want to make sure the iPad is fun and healthy for you, so just check with me first, okay?"

To Greg (thirteen): "Greg, I saw this really disturbing picture on Twitter today of the Boston Marathon bombings. Did you see it? Do you think it's real or doctored? I don't know why anyone would post that. I feel so bad for the families and having that picture go viral probably doesn't help. Why do people share such intense stuff online? Even if it isn't real, it's hard for me to get that image out of my head. Does that happen to you? Have you seen something like that before?"

So much current discussion revolves around young children and technology. In a post from the Campaign for a Commercial-Free Childhood (CCFC) titled "Laps, Not Apps," it was stated that in the summer of 2013 the CCFC filed Federal Trade Commission complaints against two popular children's product companies that

> market their popular tablet and smart phone apps for babies as educational. The complaints build on our ongoing—and highly successful—campaign to hold the so-called "genus baby" industry accountable for false and deceptive marketing. . . . Both companies claim that their mobile apps will teach babies skills and information—including words and numbers—but neither company offers any evidence to back up their claims. To date, not a single credible scientific study has shown that babies can acquire language or math skills from interacting with screens. In addition, screen time may be harmful for babies. Research links infant screen time to sleep disturbances and delayed language acquisition, as well as problems in later childhood, such as poor school performance and childhood obesity. The American Academy of Pediatrics recommends discouraging screen time for children under two.

I can remember the urge and pressure I felt to make sure that my babies achieved and learned their ABCs and 123s at lightning speed (a syndrome that's especially common with firstborns!). When Greg was a toddler, even though we didn't have the tablets and phones we do now—just a decade later—we purchased learning games and handheld computer-like toys for "early readers" because of their promises to help us grow the best possible child. Who wouldn't want that? I mean, if a three-year-old Greg could memorize the locations of all fifty states before preschool, how could he ever be stopped? But he didn't. He just took the little stylus and jabbed it against the page until it said over and over: "Maine-Maine-Texas-Texas-Texas-Florida." Every once in a while he'd locate Oklahoma or Kentucky and we'd scream, "Genius!" And then he moved on from the expensive talking learning toy to the basic wooden blocks and superhero costumes in no time.

And now there is so much available to our wee ones in portable electronic form. If we let our young children bring their Kindles and iPods everywhere—restaurants, family visits, daily car rides—when they're young, it will be much harder to break that cycle when they're older and using the technology with more independence. There is nothing wrong with saying to a seven-year-old, "The Kindle stays home when we go over to Nana's house. I want to make sure we're visiting and not gaming." I know it's easier to give them a distraction—believe me! I'm not saying that we don't pass our kids our iPhones now and then to play a game, but it would be a major exception for a special circumstance or privilege for this to happen. Even during their worst meltdowns, in the longest lines, and during the most boring experiences, we need to see it as life experience, something our children must learn—that the world can't always be comfortable, catering to and entertaining us.

My best friend recently talked about taking her babies to the playground in a suburb of New York City. She said, "Janell, everyone is on their phones while pushing their babies on the swings, sitting on a bench by the sandbox, or enjoying their time at the park. It's just the way it is. People are working from home a lot and trying to be in both places. It's hard to talk to anyone because you feel like you're interrupting." I hate this reality, but I've noticed it too. Recently I was picking my girls up from school and most of the parents around me were waiting for dismissal with their heads down, looking at their phones. I'm sure some of them were trying to squeeze out the last few e-mails of their workday or responding to a friend or family member about something meaningful. But I can't help but think that they are missing all of these people around them. Maybe they could make a connection for a play-date for their daughter to support a budding in-class friendship, meet another family that lives in their neighborhood, or chat about a teacher they just met.

The technology has infiltrated our lives so fast. And I know that we all do it, even when it isn't meaningful. Well, at least I do it. Whenever there is a down minute at work or home or while I'm waiting for my latte, I'm checking my phone—scrolling, texting, searching—with

 Slow Tech Parenting Practice

Go somewhere or do something with the kids that isn't at the top of their list—run errands, have a conversation with another adult, go to that dentist appointment you keep canceling. Leave electronic devices at home or in the car (yours too!), and this will eliminate conversation about usage, because there's no option for it. Then watch. I bet one of the following will happen: You'll have a conversation with each other or someone new, they'll pick up a book or magazine or start doodling with the pencil and notepad buried at the bottom of your pocketbook, they'll make up a game like hand clapping or I Spy and start playing. I'm *not* saying they won't pull each other's hair or whine. I am saying learning how to keep busy, be patient, and behave is important. I am also saying that this will require more parenting skill and energy than handing them your phone does. But it's a good way to practice, and soon you'll all be pros.

no purpose. It's a habit I've worked really hard to improve on. When I want to reach for my phone during a down minute, I now ask myself questions like "Who can I start a conversation with in this line?" or "Can I just sit here? Is that okay?" Technology has become a pacifier for so many of us, used to soothe any downtime. So what aren't we doing or seeing when we're heads-down? Try leaving your phone in the car while running errands or turning it off while you're fixing dinner for the kids. It's amazing, the need to satisfy that habit! Fighting it is also setting a good example for our kids.

Recently I was in a local café having lunch with my mom. There was a family of four having lunch at the table behind us. The little boy was probably four years old. He sat at the table with earbuds in, an iPad propped up in front of him, watching a movie. The dad was reading a newspaper, rocking the baby girl's stroller while she napped. Mom was reading a book. When I see scenes like this, I try to approach it nonjudgmentally (not easy!) and imagine a scenario in which I can accept it: *We live in a tourist destination, so maybe they just traveled here from far away and needed to eat and have a break from each other. Maybe the little boy has sensory issues that make this noisy restaurant too much for him to handle.* And then the totally exhausted mother in me says that no matter what their situation is, *Good for them! They look relaxed and everyone seems satisfied. What's wrong with enjoying a silent lunch?*

But I can't move on because even if there are special circumstances for this family today, I've seen this scenario many times. And what I'm really afraid of is that the world is happening around this child—sights, sounds, people, sunshine—and he's plugged in, cut off from fully experiencing it. In the one hour I observed this family, the parents never spoke to each other, never spoke to their boy, and the boy never took his earbuds out. I would rather sit near a squirming, imperfect child who is learning how to interact, behave, and engage than a silent zombie! Risk it! Unplug your babies and bring them fully into the world!

iRule Tip: Before purchasing my son an iPhone, I assessed his maturity and asked myself, "Is he ready to handle this? Is he able to live within my boundaries without a major struggle?" This is a key question in evaluating the readiness of your child for any technology—a Kindle Fire, a Nintendo DS, a television program, a social networking account, and more.

Sample Questions

- Are household chores being done?
- Are grades up to our family's standards?
- Are responsibilities being met?
- Do we currently struggle over technology, apps, sites, etc., before I allow something new?
- Will this new technology bring our household more struggle than joy?
- Am I doing this just because all of my child's peers have it?
- How will my child use this technology? Is having it a necessity or a privilege?

iRule: Passwords

My iRule: I will always know the password.

Being in tune with our children means we understand that their behaviors and actions are trying to tell us something. Naturally, open dialogue between parent and child is best when you want to check in or take the temperature of a situation. But online, social networking sites, group texts, and privacy settings can make the technology a private world for our children. Knowing the passwords on technology accounts is a clear opportunity to provide protection in an often unpoliced world of social networking and online activities. This is not coming from a place of fear, but rather from a place of guidance. As parents, we do have the right to access our children's online world, especially as they first enter cyberspace. We are their teachers and it is important to stay in tune, talk, and guide.

Like most parents, my highest priority is the physical and emotional health of my children—as I say to my kids, I can protect you and respect you. So what does that mean and how does that look? First of all, I know my child (I will speak about Greg here, because no one else has a device of their very own for social networking just yet). I trust him to follow his own instincts and to follow the guidelines we have provided as a family. I know how he behaves and what is typical of him—what he likes, how he acts, how he talks, what interests he likes to share, etc. Second, I know his friends. I know who drives him nuts and who cracks him up and whom he really counts on. I know this because I have watched the friendships blossom and evolve. I also know this because I listen to him as he talks to me about his social relationships by relating stories and examples from his everyday life. Third, I trust my parenting instincts. I trust that I would observe when something—positive or negative—was going on with him. My hope is that either Adam or I would be able to reach him long before I would need to troll his online accounts seeking answers. But still, I want to reserve my parental right to access his online accounts in the event that I couldn't know, for one reason or another, that what he needed was parental support and involvement.

I believe that I would never intentionally cross a boundary that would violate my child's right to have a typical, age-appropriate conversation. If I should see a text conversation between Greg and one of the girls in his class and it appears to be casual and harmless, I would never continue reading. If he shares something with me that occurred online or I happen upon an exchange on Twitter, it wouldn't go any further than that very screen. I have no interest in "catching" him or embarrassing him. He can trust me. And he knows that, truly. Hell, I'm writing an ENTIRE BOOK about his tech life, and when I asked him if he wants to proofread the whole thing or at least the excerpts that involve him, he said, "I trust you, Mom. It's cool."

But I do believe that tech monitoring can be an important tool for families. Perhaps your child is a risk taker by nature. Perhaps your child was given social networking accounts at a very young age because her older siblings had it and it only seemed fair. Perhaps you have had issues in the past with inappropriate behavior or iRules violations and your child needs to be closely monitored for safety and to rebuild trust. Tech monitoring can apply to multiple scenarios in parenting. Do you notice a change in the behavior of your child or teen? Is there a big upcoming event being talked about? Are grades slipping? In one scroll through my son's Twitter account I can see what's happening for him and his peers. Some parents might be horrified if they saw the way their children post or their online interests. One fourteen-year-old girl talks incessantly about excessive dieting and exercise. Another peer retweets references to alcohol and drugs. Shifts in our children's behavior and their health and wellness happen gradually, and keeping them safe depends on our being present both in person and in cyberspace. Monitoring some peer interactions can provide insight when navigating the often chaotic waters of parenting adolescents. Beyond that, it is important to know whom our children are talking to—just like you want to know whom they hang out with away from the screens! It is important to be a known presence in the technology our children are using.

When the original iRules contract I wrote for Gregory last winter went viral, it got a lot of local attention. One of my favorite unanticipated

 ## An iPhone Fail

As I write this, there has only been one occasion when Greg violated our iRules contract. I watched as he and his close friend, June, teased each over an Instagram picture. He called her "slutty" and she called him an "ass" in the comments. It went back and forth like this for several lines, and it bothered me. He seemed too casual in his banter, cocky even, like he was pushing some boundaries. Before inflicting the loss-of-iPhone consequence, I asked him some questions.

Me: Hey, Greg, I saw your conversation with June on Instagram.

Greg: Yeah?

Me: I didn't love the language you were using.

Greg: Come on, Mom, we were joking.

Me: How would I know that? It looked pretty serious.

Greg: Yeah, but you know she's my friend. You know we were joking.

results of the contract craze was that every boy and girl interacting with Greg online learned our family standards. There were far fewer late-night texts when he turned his phone on every morning, because his peers were aware that we were "around" the technology and that the behavior related to technology use in our home was respectful. Obviously, not every family will be able to publicly share their iRules like we did, but the takeaway is that when you have clear standards for your family and hold to them, most people will respect your beliefs and rules.

A survey done in 2012 by the marketing research company Lab42 that questioned parents with children who were on social networking

Me: Maybe I know that. But it was public. Every one of her followers and every one of your followers could see it. What if people thought you made a habit of calling girls "slutty"? It wasn't a private text message or some in-person joking. You posted it for everyone to see.

Greg: Mom, no one cares.

Me: Okay, would you have said that in front of her parents? What if her parents read it? How would you feel then?

Greg: *Silence.* I guess I never thought of that. *More silence.* I would feel really dumb and embarrassed. I should erase the conversation.

Me: Okay, just keep that stuff in mind when you're posting. I'm going to keep your iPhone for the rest of the week so you can think about this.

sites found that 92 percent of parents are friends with their kids on Facebook and 72 percent of parents know their children's Facebook passwords. That's a majority. And that's a stat we can feel good about. But do we know if the password gets changed? Is it the same password for Twitter and Instagram? Do we know the screen-lock password for the phone? Knowing the passwords for all devices and accounts is a good first step for basic online guidance, especially when our children are just starting out on the technology.

Often when I lead a workshop or discussion, I walk away having learned something from the people in attendance. Recently a mother of teenage daughters said that in her home, they have a password logbook. It's a simple notebook that lists account user names along with the passwords. It's not formal or forced, just part of their family culture. I loved this idea as a simple tool to keep passwords current and accessible without fuss in a central location. Mom and Dad both keep their passwords in the logbook as well, as a sign of respect for and trust in the whole family.

Blame Me!

When I was growing up, my mother and I used to have this agreement that if I needed to get out of a situation or didn't want to take part in some behavior that I thought was risky, but wasn't sure how to assert myself, I could "blame" her. I could tell my friends, "My mom is so mean, I have to go home now." Or "My mom won't let me go. She is so strict." I say the same thing to Greg now—blame me! If you need an out, use me! I would rather you tell everyone I'm the evilist beast than have you do something you're not sure about.

Parent Story

One of my favorite stories from a one-on-one parent coaching session is that of Jimmy. Jimmy's a popular fifteen-year-old high school freshman.

His mother, Maggie, set up an appointment with me to discuss a situation that played out in her house. It was a busy summer and she hadn't really been checking up on Jimmy's online behavior. He has a smartphone, and they don't usually have a lot of struggles over his use of it. Maggie knows Jimmy's a good kid, a good student, and that he's had the same group of friends since preschool. For about a week, she had noticed that Jimmy was moody and cranky—a door was slammed, he had an attitude and lacked motivation—but she figured he was tired and it was a phase. During the school year, Maggie knows Jimmy's passwords and scrolls through his phone on a weekly basis. But this summer, she hadn't been as diligent. Finally, one afternoon they started to argue about chores. Maggie asked, "What is going on with you? I'm tired of the attitude. I'm going to keep your phone until you get your chores done." Jimmy snapped back, "Why don't you take a look at my phone while you have it? Be prepared to see some stuff you don't like." And he stormed away. And then the lightbulb went on for Maggie. Something had been brewing online that was causing her son to act out. She realized that he must have been dealing with something pretty intense for him to tell her to read through his phone messages. So she took some time, logged in, and went through the past few weeks of text conversations and social networking interactions. It seemed that he was being targeted by a couple of boys he doesn't hang out with.

They started by texting him from a few different numbers he didn't recognize. They didn't reply when he asked, "Who is this?" They made sexually explicit comments about his girlfriend: "I'm with her right now and we're [doing x]." He lashed out in the same vulgar tone, demanding that the texts stop and the aggressors shut up. But this just escalated the situation and it lasted for more than a week, growing very intense at points. There was also texting between Jimmy and his girlfriend. He was defensive, asking her if she was hanging out with anyone. There was a sense of helplessness in the content, especially since Jimmy could only speculate about who had been texting him. Should he be mad at her? Should he stand up for her? Was he playing the fool?

This sense of isolation and confusion was clearly a lot for a young teenager (or anyone!) to deal with alone. It certainly explained why Jimmy's behavior had been so erratic. Remember when our kids were little and they would start to cry or fuss and we would know they were tired or teething? Their behavior was telling us something. It's the same way for tweens and teens. When they act out or slam a door, we know there's more to the story. That's a great time to get curious and ask some questions. So after reviewing the online conversations, Maggie understood what Jimmy had been dealing with. So what happened next?

First, Maggie felt happy that, even if it took a week, Jimmy came to her. He basically said, "Please read this and help me navigate through it." Well, maybe not that exactly, but as parents, we believe that our kids need our help all the time and that once we have the information we need, we can save the world. True or not, it keeps us going every day. Either way, he wanted her to see it.

Then she got mad at herself. She knew better than to let so much time pass without checking his phone. He'd probably been coping with a lot, and she'd had no idea. Parent Guilt (yes, with a capital G)—if we had had the information sooner, we could have protected our beloved child from harm.

Then she got mad at those fresh boys that were harassing her son. She suspected she knew who they were and thought it was "typical" of those kids, the punks.

Then she was horrified that her own son used the language he did to retaliate. (Actually, she thought some of his comebacks were really good! But he could never know that.)

After we processed all of this, Maggie understood that she needed to have a conversation with her son. This situation was a major door opener for their relationship. She could not flip out. She could not act horrified. She needed to be a voice of reason and a person that could guide her child in problem solving. I encouraged Maggie to sit with Jimmy. To let him know that she had read the conversations and knew what was going on. To ask him to tell his version of the whole story, because perhaps there were pieces that took place away from the virtual world. Maggie wanted me to tell her what she could teach Jimmy to do next time.

There is no perfect answer. Our hope as parents is that we have the pulse of these happenings by being present on the technology, that we actually see a conversation like this before it becomes too big. Our next hope is that if we don't see it, our children come to us with it: "I don't know who's texting me. I don't know what I should say." Perhaps we hope that our child uses silence so as not to fuel the conflict, simply making no response at all. Most people that are looking to tease or taunt will stop if the other person doesn't "play." Also, I tell Greg and parents in my workshops that if a conversation is happening online and it gets

Believe It or Not

Our kids want us to be present! They don't want us to be in the dark, they want us to understand. It makes them feel safe and guided. They want limits and boundaries as tools to help them learn their way through the world. Does it get any better than an environment where children can make mistakes, take age-appropriate risks for growth, and be corrected with guidance while knowing they are unconditionally loved? The truth is, they might not say this—ever. Assume it. Own the idea that you will make your child feel better when you have a tech presence and understanding.

uncomfortable or you don't want it to go any further, use a simple statement like "I'm not talking to you about this over text." It is a powerful tool
that either changes the subject or ends the conversation.

After our session together, Maggie had renewed her belief that
checking in with our kids and our kids' screens is vital to building
healthy behaviors and relationships with technology. Again, knowing
passwords promotes our duty to "protect and respect," it is not a violation of our children's privacy. As we closed our conversation, I heard
confidence return to Maggie's voice. She knows what's important to
her family and what standards of behavior are acceptable in her house
and on their phones. Certainly, this would not be the last situation that
required support or guidance for Jimmy. But now Maggie had the
assurance she needed to guide her family.

How to Avoid Being a Creeper

When Instagram was new on the scene a few years ago, I allowed Greg
to get an account on his device, an iPod Touch. I too got an Instagram
account. At this time I was leading a summer teen leadership program
Greg and many of his peers were involved in. One day he posted a
picture and a few of the teens commented about something genuinely funny. I knew it was genuinely funny and innocent because I had
witnessed it! I was there with them! So I decided to comment, "For real!
Lol!" Almost immediately Gregory came to me. "Mom, no. Stop, don't
comment. It's not funny. You're not funny. That's being a creeper."
Ouch. I was hurt. I am funny and cool! And I knew these kids; it was my
business too. Except it wasn't my business, and I shouldn't try to be
funny or cool to a group of my son's friends even if I work closely with
them every day. I could see something online and talk about it to my
son in person—we do this all the time: "Her comment was really
funny," or "Do you think it was a good idea for him to post that picture?"—but publicly, I needed to keep quiet.

A creeper is defined in a contemporary slang dictionary as someone who views your online profile multiple times. A creeper is described as both a nonposting lurker or stalker and someone that is constantly commenting, trolling, and getting involved in, well, a creepy way. Creepers are usually peers and are not looked upon favorably. But then there are "parent creepers." A parent creeper doesn't just monitor their own children, they monitor everyone's. They scroll online to be up on the gossip and the business of teens. They like being "in the know." Sometimes parent creepers may even text or communicate with the teens in an attempt to relate to or befriend them in cases of teenage drama or confusion. Parent creepers often seem like they are concerned or trying to help, but we need to be cautious about how we're mixing with our children's peers. How involved are we in the relationships? What is our role? There is a real difference between being an adult whom children can trust and acting like a child or teen. Being a parent creeper can have a negative effect on your relationship with your child. Make sure there are clear boundaries on what the expectation is for peer–parent communication. Overdoing it can potentially damage trust and sabotage the chance of a child respecting their iRules rather than resenting them. Here are some suggestions for how to avoid creeping but still preserve an online parental presence. I describe this balance as being "on it," not "in it."

On It—Not in It

○ Always ask older children for their okay before posting or tagging photos of them. Ask that they do the same for you to practice and teach mutual respect.

○ Limit public comments on their posts and pictures.

○ Limit the amount of trolling you do for no reason. The slang for this is "creeping" to find out other people's business just for the sake of knowing it.

- ○ Limit commenting on the posts of their peers, even if the peers chose to follow or friend you first.
- ○ Don't obsess over their everyday convos; keep your antennae up for real health and safety concerns, and when they come up, don't hesitate to step in.

Don't Panic!

- ○ If you are offended or confused by or unsure of something you see online, talk about it face-to-face with your child. Most inappropriate behavior can be resolved with an offline conversation. If it doesn't directly involve your child, still have the discussion. These moments are the most teachable because the emotional temperature tends to be lower.
- ○ Make sure your children know that online posts, texts, and e-mails are not truly private. They can be shared and viewed by the masses with ease. Do not allow them to believe in a false sense of trust or privacy online. This will help them make better choices on their own, limiting your need to creep.
- ○ Think about how and when you would step in and speak up offline and apply those same boundaries to the screen. If you are consistent in your parenting online and offline, your children will feel secure because they are already familiar with your expectations and will be less likely to feel invaded or violated.

The Problem with Passwords

When my iRules contract went viral, this password contract point was one of the most controversial. Privacy and protection are emotionally charged subjects because they bring up the values of trust and honesty. When I've spoken to other parents about this, one mother of a large family told me she firmly believes that children living in her house do not have a right to privacy. Another mother of a teenage daughter said knowing her child's password would be like reading her diary, a violation of privacy that she would never contemplate. I received an e-mail from a mother across the country that told me she trusts her daughter, but doesn't trust anyone else because her daughter was deceived by a person she'd never met, and that having the password would have helped the mother navigate through the situation sooner and with less struggle. I've also received so much feedback from teens and parents saying that I don't trust Greg and that knowing the passwords means I want to spy. We all have different views on privacy and passwords. What's right will be clearer for some and more of a challenge for others. Always come back to your instincts and stand up for what feels right according to your beliefs in your household. For me, I always come back to this one central principle: "If I might need a password, I want to have it."

And what about the times when knowing the password is not enough? I have heard several stories about cousins or aunts seeing actions by their younger relatives online. One young woman shared, "I found out that one of my cousins in middle school had an Instagram account and was begging strangers to follow her. I found it completely alarming, so I took a screenshot and sent it to my mother and uncle for parent intervention. I lost my title as 'cool cousin,' but I would rather have her understand the importance of strangers and safe chatting. My other cousins told their dad they did not have a Facebook account. And even though he monitors the family computer, they had the app hidden in a folder and he had no idea."

My sister Kellie is twenty-five, and she is very close to my kids. We have an agreement that if she sees something one of my kids (only Gregory at this point) does online and thinks it's "not right," she can talk to them directly about it. Hopefully they will respect her enough to make the change she's suggesting. But if she sees something that is dangerous or requires immediate intervention and attention, she must come to me (or Adam) without question. She will always be cool in

Gregory's eyes because he's aware that she has his well-being in mind above all. Gregory knows about and understands this agreement too. We all need people we can trust and people our kids can trust as support. Encourage the people in your life to be models and guides for your children online. And if they can't be guides because of their own inappropriate behavior, let them be a lesson!

Simply knowing passwords is not a strong enough strategy for online safety. Conversations with your child need to be clear and direct about your expectations for their online behavior. Risks need to be defined and discussed. Honesty between parent and child must be honored. And consequences need to be enforced, especially if our children are playing with fire online. Knowing passwords is passive parenting, just a piece of the pie. But parenting technology is an active effort requiring the development of iRules and continued conversations as we experience the technology and get to know our children and their tendencies.

Privacy: Defined

So what does tech privacy look like in my house? Greg can have private conversations; he can FaceTime from behind a closed door or text whomever he likes as long as it's a person he has met face-to-face. I do not need to read every detail. And I don't want to! But I might ask, "Who have you been texting with lately?" I usually do a weekly check-in and reserve the right to take the "temperature" of the online climate he is in. But honestly, some weeks I don't. A lot of the conversations we have as a family dictate or set the stage for his online behaviors. I put a lot of trust in that. The same rules apply to online gaming. The central question is "Would we invite the person you are playing with into our living room or to play in the backyard?" If not, he needs permission.

Also, in other parts of Greg's life, he is trustworthy. By nature, he doesn't lie or sneak or cheat. He is mature for his age. He is comfortable with who he is. He can communicate his needs. He's always where he is supposed to be when he isn't home. I know his friends. I know where he goes. And the way I see him is consistent with the feedback I get from teachers, coaches, and other parents. So why does all of this matter when it comes to privacy and technology? Greg's everyday life and behaviors show me what his tendencies with the technology are. They don't tell me everything—technology allows more freedom, it can be more isolated, it's easier to take risks or be impulsive. But I have insight from my children's everyday lives that will help me determine how much space I can give. If I give Greg a little wiggle room and he meets my expectations on his own, then great! This is the goal—to eventually have raised our children consistently and deliberately enough that they naturally follow their own inner compasses and boundaries. They will do what feels right to them based on what we have nurtured and taught. But if I give him that same space and don't tell him, "It's 7:30, you need to put your phone away" and he keeps it with him until 9:30, then I know he's not ready to self-monitor. He still needs my support and structure. So much of the type of parenting, privacy limits, and guidance we give are based on the individual child. Know your whole child and set them up for tech success.

Snapchat is one of the trickier social networking apps for me to parent because whatever Greg sends or receives disappears after ten seconds. I know he sends goofy, horrible, close-up selfies to me over Snapchat and pics of yummy food or snacks to my sister. And I'm sure I'm missing an occasional raised middle finger sent to his buddies or some other borderline behavior. But I must have faith that we've set such clear boundaries and had so many thorough conversations that he understands and follows my expectations even if I can't see what he sends.

I use a lot of examples in my discussions about online privacy. I think the one message I hear over and over again from teachers, parents, and law enforcement officials is that nothing is actually private online. We share a picture or text conversation and even if we click to delete it from our device, there is no guarantee that it actually is deleted on our screen or the screens of our peers. There are so many examples of this that we can share with our children so they don't find themselves in a difficult situation over something they assumed to be personal or private. Over and over I hear parents talk about bikini, topless, or sexual pics circulating through Snapchat and beyond. Even though it's supposed to disappear after a few seconds, a screenshot of it can be saved to any device. The girls involved in taking and sending the pictures think they will remain private. The boys involved often share and save without thinking about the consequences. Discussing the privacy aspects of the technology provides us with opportunities to support our children. We can speak to how unfortunate it is to watch a young girl make the harmful decision to share sexual photos of herself, and we can also speak to the idea that even if she intends for them to be private, privacy just doesn't exist. We can also talk firmly to boys about the responsibility they have to act properly. Be clear and direct with your son about the way you would like him to handle the situation should he receive a sexual picture.

When I ask families what single rule on their iRules contract they want their children (no matter what their age) to hear loud and clear, it is almost always some version of this: "Nothing you say or do online is private." So what does your child's "privacy" mean for you? Having a list of their followers? Scrolling through their e-mails and texts every day? Prohibiting social networking accounts? Having free access to their pictures? Your idea of it might be very different from mine. We need to assess our own definitions and expectations of privacy, couple that with our children's tendencies, and balance the two. We don't have to either allow total freedom or hound our children on their every online move. Know the needs of your family!

And what about our nonteens? Even though Brendan has limited access to his iPod Touch, he is eager to have something all his own and loves having a password to keep his sisters from gaming or listening to music on it. And while most days I know his password, he loves to change it, and the girls love to try and figure it out. Sometimes he'll choose one of them and "allow" them to know the sacred password— a typical example of the torturous relationships among siblings. This is Brendan's expression of power over his younger siblings. You locked your diary, right? You had a KEEP OUT sign on your bedroom door? It feels the same way. Because I know the apps he has and that he has no social networking accounts, he does not text, and he uses the device very infrequently, I'm not concerned about his password. But when he starts to interact with peers online, share photos, and expand his virtual use beyond our own home, I will require his password. Also, if your elementary school–age child has an e-reader, a portable electronic device, or video game accounts with passwords to keep information private from you or if you detect sneaky behaviors, make it easy and do not allow passwords! Treat your child's password like you would a bedroom door—you may knock before entering, but you would never allow them to lock you out indefinitely.

Another important discussion to have about passwords is the way in which we share them. A key nonnegotiable rule should be that passwords are private for families! Advise your children to never share their passwords for e-mail or social networking accounts or for their phone lock with friends. One teenage girl I heard about had trusted some peers with her passwords and they went into her phone and a few of her accounts and made comments, texted, and created havoc. Sometimes sharing passwords can be used as a (faux) sign of friendship and loyalty. Sometimes the password peer pressure can look like this: "If we are really best friends and you trust me, then tell me your password. I swear I won't use it or tell anyone!" Beyond peer relationships, our kids should also know that no one outside the family—especially another adult—should ask for or need their password for any reason. Adults must talk to adults, it's that easy. Create some boundaries like these to help your children safely navigate a world of passwords.

A set of family iRules will balance privacy and protection for our children so we can allow them to explore their independence within the boundaries that satisfy our parenting limits. Taking preventive measures like knowing the passwords or disabling passwords helps kids establish good tech habits and can be modified for all ages, personalities, and needs.

iRule Tip: List all of the online accounts your child has. Do you have the passwords to these accounts? Do you understand how to navigate through and operate each account and activity in the event that you need to access it? If not, learn to use the technology that your children use. Be present in these places. If your child is on Twitter, get a Twitter account. Follow each other. Have a presence in the technology just like you would have a presence away from the technology.

iRule: Sleep First

> **My iRule:** Hand the phone to one of your parents promptly at 7:30 p.m. every school night and every weekend night at 9:00 p.m. It will be shut off for the night and turned on again at 7:30 a.m. If you would not make a call to someone's landline because their parents might answer first, then do not call or text. Listen to those instincts and respect other families like we would like to be respected.

Setting an iRule concerning sleep is crucial. One of the biggest problems we had immediately with Gregory's iPhone was group texts. One morning when Greg woke up and turned his phone back on, he had 672 text message notifications. I was in total disbelief. It was a weeknight and the last text he received was sent at 2:30 a.m. and the first of the next day was at 6:30 a.m. I was shocked. I could only imagine that if I hadn't set this rule for him and he had brought his phone into his bedroom, his sleep would have been interrupted by vibrating notifications hundreds of times. Not to mention that Gregory and Brendan share a room, so even my then fourth-grader would have felt the consequences of disrupted sleep. Sleep felt like one of the more urgent things I needed to protect for my growing adolescent.*

---

*It's no wonder that anything possibly disrupting the sleep of any of us would feel urgent to me—especially after having had five newborns in eight years. A mama's got to protect what's precious!

When I talk to teens and young adults, I often hear "My phone's my alarm clock" or "My phone helps me fall asleep." But when we discuss it a little further, one of the consistent themes is that they're afraid that if they don't sleep with their phones, they will "miss out" or "something terrible might happen." Below are excerpts from conversations I've had with young people that keep their phones close by overnight.

○ *When I got my cell phone, my family had a lot of issues at the time. I kept my phone on [when I was away at college] just in case I needed to rush home in the middle of the night. Now I leave it on for anyone who needs support, a ride, or just someone to talk to.*

○ *I feel like I will miss out on something if I am disconnected from it. Whether it's a text message or a Facebook update, I think it's comforting to "be in the know" on what's going on in my world and the world of my peers.*

○ *I have found, especially recently, that people expect you to have your phone on you at all times. If a friend or a family member or my boyfriend calls me and I don't answer, they automatically assume something is wrong and then text me several times asking, "Are you okay?" or saying, "Pick up your phone!"*

○ *I have a bad nightly routine of looking at social media and random Web sites in bed before I go to sleep and I'm just lazy and don't turn it off.*

○ *I leave my phone on me all the time, so I have the constant communication with me at all times. I find it sickening, yet I cannot stop. When my iPhone glass once broke and I was unable to use it and had to wait three days for a new one to come in the mail, I felt lost.*

I think these responses speak to our attachment to our devices and how central social networking and online communication have become. The value of setting an iRule curfew for technology use was confirmed when I attended a lecture led by a pediatrician about teens and sleep. He believed that inconsistent and disrupted sleep was causing many concentration and health problems for our children. He pleaded with parents to do whatever they could to nurture a healthy sleeping environment. The 2011 annual poll conducted for the National Sleep Foundation found that about two-thirds of teens between the ages of thirteen and eighteen used their computers, laptops, and/or cell phones within the hour before going to bed. And a good portion of those teens said that a text message, phone call, or e-mail had woken them up a few nights per week.

Define a healthy sleep environment for your family. For our family, the cure is to turn the devices off for the night at least an hour before bed. When we use electronic devices, the brain is stimulated, it's called to action. Have you ever experienced this? When I was writing and researching this book, I was chronically using my computer, iPad, and smartphone (ironic, right?) to gather information, watch documentaries, converse with people, and read. Just around the time I started to spend more evenings with my devices, I started to experience restless sleep. As a person that usually falls asleep and stays asleep with ease, I was buzzing when I turned the lights out. I was also waking up multiple times during the night, thinking about what I had seen or heard. Now I'm aware that I had deadlines approaching and speaking engagements to prepare for and they were all very important to me and at the forefront of my consciousness. And yes, I probably would have tossed and turned a bit more than usual due to my excitement anyway. But I don't think the technology helped. So I enforced the same rule for myself that I have for my kiddos. I started turning my devices off at least an hour before I went to bed. I stopped reading e-books and looking at videos. I didn't play Boggle until I fell asleep. I just stopped the late-night tech use. And I slept more soundly when I made this small shift. I could feel my mind calm down.

I thought about children and teens during the months I was overdosing on tech. I remembered growing up and everything feeling so important—sports, social life, romance, schoolwork, parents, conflict. It was all so central, it probably occupied as much space in my teenage mind as my professional life does in my adult mind now. So what would it have felt like to bring my teenage world, filled with ups and downs, into my room with me every night? What if I put it right next to my bed, letting it chirp at me, never leaving me alone? I started to advise many of the parents I coach to have the child unplug and be away from it for the night.

Preserving a full night's sleep for our children is Slow Tech Parenting at its finest. Getting enough sleep is critical for a child's development, and it must be considered sacred. We all deserve to crawl into bed, spend some time alone reflecting, put the day behind us, and fall asleep. As a child and teenager, I always read before I fell asleep. That has become a lifelong ritual for me—a gift, really. On the other hand, Brendan and Gregory share a room. One of my favorite demonstrations of their brotherly bond is listening to their nightly conversations as they are falling asleep: *Who's the best NBA player? Did you see my goal during soccer today? What's the middle school bus ride like? Who's your favorite* SNL *character?*

So if our children and teens are scrolling through social networking sites while lying in bed, what aren't they doing instead? What is being lost? A chapter of a book? A conversation with a sibling? A chance to imagine or drift? This may seem inconsequential, but I believe these are the moments and experiences we need to protect the most.

Good Night, iPhone!

Every weeknight during the school year, when 7:30 strikes I ask Greg to finish his conversations, wrap up what he's doing, and turn the phone off. He puts the phone on our kitchen counter—a central location in our house—and leaves it charging overnight. He doesn't use the phone again until the next morning. This rule is clear, concise, and nonnegotiable. And it works without issue! Sweet dreams without disruption.

This iRule gets referenced a lot in my workshops. Parents want to know *how* I get him to put away his phone. This question is tricky for me because honestly, I'm wondering when he will start to fight this one. We are one year into his iPhone ownership, and this has never been a problem. He has asked for a few more minutes here and there to finish a conversation, but that's it. Here are a few of my thoughts on the reasons behind the "non-struggle" over unplugging for the night.

1. He gets to hang out with Adam and me solo because his younger siblings are already up in bed.

2. He's tired from a full day of school and sports.

3. He doesn't have anything else to say to his peers.

 # Excuse-Proof Yourself

Here are some of the most common excuses I hear when talking with parents and kids alike about having their phones in their bedrooms.

- O It's my alarm clock. *Get an alarm clock.*
- O Knowing it's right there helps me sleep. *That's a bad habit.*
- O What if someone needs me? *It can wait until morning.*
- O I want to listen to music. *Get a radio. (Get a radio alarm clock—two birds, one stone!)*
- O It doesn't wake me up. *Yes, it does, even if you don't realize it.*
- O I read on it. *Get a book.*
- O I like playing games before bed. *Get some crossword puzzles.*
- O I put it on DO NOT DISTURB. *Great! It won't disturb you when you put it in a central location either.*

Developing healthy sleep patterns requires that technology be turned off for an extended time before bed, devices be banned from the bedroom, and bedtime and waking time be consistent.

LIAR! Okay, the Whole Truth . . .

I love to play soothing music on the iPad as bedtime music for my girls in their bedrooms and also did this for my boys when they were younger. The difference in using the technology this way is that they're not responding to texts, surfing the 'Net, or jamming in earbuds while they're falling asleep. They are just listening and experiencing the music. When I go to bed, I turn it off. Evaluate and assess the acceptability of tech use for different scenarios in your house! This proves I'm flexible, right?!

The Loss of Landline

When I was growing up and wanted to call a friend or a crush, I had to be brave enough to call their home, a place where their parents might answer! Prior to dialing, whether I realized it or not, I had to ask myself some version of the following:

- How do I want to sound? Polite? Rude? Quiet? Nervous? Confident?
- Is it too late at night?
- Is it too early in the morning?
- Is it a good time to call or am I too giggly because I'm at a sleepover with eight other twelve-year-old girls?
- Do I want to leave a message on the family's answering machine that will be played for all to hear upon their return home?
- Have I already called today and not gotten a call back? Do I want to be a stalker?

O   Will I be able to handle a conversation if the phone's answered by the person's mom, dad, or older brother, who all make me nervous?

O   Is there a risk that I might hang up because I'm not ready with what I want to say?

O   What is my motive for calling? What do I want to say to the person if they're actually home?

With these questions came some form of anticipation or preparedness to evaluate the purpose of the phone call. I am certain that my peers were likewise running through similar questions before they called my home. On more than one occasion, my father answered the phone and I heard him say, "It's too late. She can't talk." And that was that. There was no other access to me.

Now we must teach our children to use those same standards despite the ease of use and constant contact permitted by cell phones. Parents need to keep talking to each other too! Having personal relationships with other parents makes knowing and respecting each other's technology rules easier, so introduce yourself, ask permission, confirm plans, say thank you, and take all opportunities to connect face to face.

☑ iRule Tip: Make it easy for your child to unplug. Pull the plug! Every night, give your child a nonnegotiable time to stop using technology. At least an hour before bed is a great time to shut it all down and connect with family or have quiet time.

2

The Golden Rules

iRule: Do unto Others

My iRule: Do not use this technology to lie to, fool, or deceive another human being. Do not involve yourself in conversations that are hurtful to others. Be a good friend first or stay the hell out of the crossfire.

My iRule: Do not text, e-mail, or say anything through this device that you would not say in person.

My iRule: Do not text, e-mail, or say anything to someone that you would not say out loud with their parents in the room. Censor yourself.

This chapter is a tool that applies the golden rule to technology etiquette—how we treat one another in the electronic world. It is our obligation as parents to make certain our children handle online peer relationships with the highest integrity. This needs to be taught just as we would teach it away from the screen. This chapter explores cyberbullying, friend fail, and the power of language by discussing specific examples and the greater cultural conversations behind and research on these topics.

Cyberbullying

Note: I could literally write an entire book just on this topic. In no way is what I discuss in this section comprehensive in the scope of its research, or in the examples and explanations given. Cyberbullying is as deep and wide as a topic as it is serious. Its consequences vary from the mild to the unthinkable. Every day our school officials, law enforcement officers, legal advocates, and media figures are discussing and learning new ways to understand, prevent, and cope with it. The permanence of the technology in the lives of our children makes cyberbullying a primary source of concern for families. Here I hope to bring you a clearer understanding of cyberbullying and the courage to use some basic tools to bring the conversation to your kitchen table, where it will not be hidden, secret, or misunderstood, but rather the topic of an ongoing, comfortable family discussion.

According to StopCyberbullying.org, cyberbullying is

> when a child, preteen or teen is tormented, threatened, harassed, humiliated, embarrassed or otherwise targeted by another child, preteen or teen using the Internet, interactive and digital technologies or mobile phones. It has to have a minor on both sides, or at least [to] have been instigated by a minor against another minor.

Like bullying away from the screen, cyberbullying is a power play. It is deliberate and chronic. But according to DoSomething.org, 81 percent of young people think that cyberbullying is easier to get away with than bullying in person. This is because it is often hidden from others, perpetrated away from school, or anonymous, and because the bully doesn't see the victim's emotional reaction. DoSomething.org also reports that only 10 percent of victims will turn to a parent or trusted adult for help. This list of examples of cyberbullying comes from the Web site of the National Crime Prevention Council (NCPC).

O   Sending someone mean or threatening e-mails, instant messages, or text messages

O   Excluding someone from an instant messenger buddy list or blocking their e-mail for no reason

O   Tricking someone into revealing personal or embarrassing information and sending it to others

O   Breaking into someone's e-mail or instant message account to send cruel or untrue messages while posing as that person

O   Creating Web sites to make fun of another person such as a classmate or teacher

O   Using Web sites to rate peers as prettiest, ugliest, etc.

The NCPC goes on to describe the effects of these actions.

O   It occurs in the child's home. Being bullied at home can take away the place children feel most safe.

O   It can be harsher. Often kids say things online that they wouldn't say in person, mainly because they can't see the other person's reaction.

O   It can be far reaching. Kids can send e-mails making fun of someone to their entire class or school with a few clicks, or post them on a Web site for the whole world to see.

○ It can be anonymous. Cyberbullies often hide behind screen names and e-mail addresses that don't identify who they are. Not knowing who is responsible for bullying messages can add to a victim's insecurity.

○ It may seem inescapable. It may seem easy to get away from a cyberbully by just getting offline, but for some kids not going online takes away one of the major places they socialize.

Below are some real-life examples of cyberbullying that I've heard from participants in my workshops and teen empowerment groups and that I've observed among the teens I know.

○ An eighth-grade boy named Chris uses his smartphone to photograph the same female classmate, Leanne, every day during school hours. She is unpopular and often is ostracized, teased, or ignored by her peers. Most of the photos of Leanne are taken without her knowledge. She is reading a book or completing schoolwork in many of the shots. Most of the pictures are awkward or unflattering. Chris then posts the pictures of Leanne on Twitter with captions like "My girlfriend" or "So beautiful." Many of his followers like or retweet the photos and soon many peers and classmates are spreading "the joke" around social networking sites. Word spreads to Leanne, and she even sees a few of the tweets herself. She ignores them and hopes they'll go away.

○ Angie, a sixteen-year-old student athlete, is a smart, conscientious, accepted member of her high school. One day she starts receiving text messages from an unknown number. The messages say, "Hi, Angie," but there is no reply when Angie repeatedly asks, "Who is this?" or says, "Sorry, I don't know this number." Angie feels annoyed. Soon she is receiving multiple daily texts from this number with an increasing degree of sexual suggestiveness and pornographic pictures with captions like "You know you want this, Angie." She answers back "Stop!" and "Who are you?" but this seemingly just encourages the behavior and she gets replies like "You don't need to know who I am, but I know who you are, Angie." It goes on for weeks, but Angie doesn't tell her parents because she is trying to handle it herself and feels embarrassed about the content of the text messages. Anger and fear are her primary emotions for almost a month while she's being harassed. She finally decides to seek help by confiding in her parents.

O Molly is fifteen and has recently ended the relationship with her steady boyfriend, Mike. They do not go to the same school, so Molly doesn't see him around anymore. She decides to unfriend and unfollow Mike on all social networking accounts to make the breakup easier. Molly continues to post pictures of friends, sports, and other social events on her accounts. One day she receives a private Facebook message from Mike using his friend Jay's Facebook account. It reads, "Molly, you better not be dating anyone yet. Slut." She is confused and unsure of how to respond. So she says, "Stop creeping on my account. Grow up." Every few days Mike logs in to a different friend's account or sends a text message to Molly—"What will you do if I show up at your school dance this weekend?" or "I know you're going to the football game with Aaron, I'll be there too." Molly blocks all of their mutual friends' accounts and tells him to stop, but Mike always finds a way to express his need to be a presence in her life. She feels trapped because she doesn't want to get him in real trouble and thinks she might be overreacting, but she also wants him to stop.

The Challenges of Cyberbullying

O In each of these stories, the victim feels some combination of embarrassment, annoyance, shame, confusion, upset, fear, and powerlessness.

O The victims don't know protocol. Who should they talk to about this? Who is a friend in these situations?

- o The consequences for the victims are often unknown by adults and unsettling for the victims—social ostracism, fear of being a tattletale, accusations of overacting or not being able to take a joke.
- o The consequences for the offender are often scary and unsettling—punishment of varying severity, possible police involvement, inclusion in a school record, effects on the rest of the bully's life.
- o Cyberbullying happens in isolation—on phones, computers, and social networking accounts—so parents don't see it unless they go looking. In contrast, imagine a regular prank caller to your landline. The entire family would know that something was going on because the phone is often centrally located and is used by the entire family. It would be the same situation for a harassing letter or note sent to your house.

There are other ways that calculated meanness can take place online. "Subtweets," or subliminal tweets, are tweets that directly refer to a person without saying their name. For example, "Soooo awkward!" or "Why won't he notice me?" The intention to hurt can be elevated in these too—"Ur so fat" or "No friends." This is quite common and often hurtful because it takes many forms. It targets one person publicly without identifying them. But also, it leaves peers wondering, *Who is she talking about? Is it me? What did I do?* Subtweets are often retweeted and can become inside stories or jokes.

If we understand that conflict will be part of our children's online world (and offline world), we can help our children deal with it directly. Conflict is a part of life and often quite healthy. It allows one to express needs or find a solution to a problem. This is a crucial lesson that can apply both on and away from the screens. Most of the time, the actual problem happens away from the screen—at school, at a sleepover or sports event, etc.—and goes unaddressed in that setting. It is then carried online, where taunting is shielded or safe

Handling Conflict at Home

A key way to help our children identify, understand, and resolve conflict with peers is to practice strategies within the family system. Guide. Model. Explain. Talk about it.

Example: Ella is screaming at Lily and calling her names. She comes to me and tattles that Lily thinks she "owns" Ella's new puppy and that it's not fair that Lily thinks she's in charge. I want Ella to practice speaking directly to Lily about what is bothering her. I sit the girls down and the conversation looks like this.

Ella: I get mad when you wake up before me and sneak the dog out for a walk without my permission.

Lily: I wasn't sneaking. I was helping. Why were you so mean to me?

Ella: I want you to wake me up when you do, so I have a chance to walk the new puppy too. You can't hog him just because you wake up earlier.

Lily: Okay. Can I sometimes walk the puppy without you?

Ella: Maybe. But you have to ask me the night before.

It isn't perfect, but the emotional temperature has cooled. The girls are talking about the core of the conflict—power. They find some common ground and are both willing to bend a little. This is good practice for expressing themselves without yelling, name-calling, bringing up old stuff, crying, whining, or tattling. I encourage them to be as direct as they can be (considering their ages). Allowing siblings to discuss and communicate is a safe way for them to practice the skills they will need to handle conflict and emotions with their peers.

from adult monitoring. Sometimes an online conversation is misinterpreted and then weaves its way into the classrooms and hallways. Talk to your children about this. Have they experienced it? Do they know someone that has? Ask for examples. A key to understanding conflict is to identify it. Then practice resolving it. Set up different online conflict scenarios with your son or daughter and ask them how they would respond. Support them in the process. Teach them that conflict can be positive, but usually a face-to-face encounter will be most productive and reduce the risk of making a private issue public or not saying exactly what we mean. If your child feels attacked or is unsure about handling a conflict online, have them rely on that simple phrase again: "I don't want to talk about this online." When we teach our children to accept and handle conflict, we eliminate a lot of unnecessary online negativity.

Responding and Reporting

Elizabeth Englander is the director of the Massachusetts Aggression Reduction Center at Bridgewater State University. In her 2010 article "Reducing Bullying and Cyberbullying," she talks about the difference between "responding" and "reporting." When we see a behavior that we don't like, even if the behavior doesn't require us to report it to the school, another child's parents, or law enforcement, we should still express our disapproval of the behavior. All negative online behaviors require us to respond.

True Story: I scrolled through Greg's texts one night and some friends were talking about a new trend called slap cam. One of the boys said he was at a sleepover and while he was sleeping, another buddy, who was videotaping, slapped him in the face and shared it on social networking sites. This horrified me. I googled more info and found that there are thousands of examples of this trend online. So I

Parenting Ugly Truth

The night of our original slap cam discussion, Greg came to me and asked to attend a sleepover with the very same group of boys who were slap camming! Seriously?! Of course I wanted to say no, I wanted to put my foot down. I wanted to protect my boy from being smacked (literally!) out of his healthy, perfect slumbering dreams. But I couldn't! He told me that he said to his friends—and I quote—"We're not doing any of that stupid camera slapping shit. I'm going to lose it on somebody if it happens." His buddies agreed that for the most part they hated it too—they were "over it." It was hard for me to let him go to the sleepover—I offered him ice cream and a late movie instead. I kept remembering the slap (and smack) cam YouTube and Vine clips I watched of strangers. But I knew he needs to learn how to assert himself, how to deal with various situations, to navigate some of the dumbest adolescent waters of all times. I reminded him that I would speak up if I saw anything like that shared online. I carried on about the violation of privacy, the violence, the lack of respect it showed. I told him I would pick him up at any point in the night if everyone got wild. I may or may not have squealed, "Isn't anything sacred anymore? Can't kids just go to a sleepover and stay up late and not video, document, and share every ridiculous thing?!" He laughed and assured me, "Mom, it just won't happen." And he was right, it didn't. Damn, parenting and loving people can be so hard.

decided to respond within my own family even though Greg hadn't been involved. Here's my version of questions to ask in this "respond" conversation.

○ What do you know about slap cam?
○ I saw that some of the guys were talking about it in a group text. Has that ever happened to you? Have you ever done it to anyone else? Have you ever seen it happen?
○ When I googled it, I thought it was pretty intense and violent. I think it's scary and mean, not funny. Do you?
○ Why would kids do that to each other? What's the point? Do you get it when I am missing it completely?
○ I would be so upset and angry if that happened to you or to someone staying in our house. How can we make sure it doesn't?

Each question deepened the conversation. The conversation was casual and we didn't spend a lot of time on it since we basically had the same point of view. But I felt like he understood my expectations and had had a place to express his thoughts too.

Responding allows us to actively parent before an occurrence directly involves our child. We discuss our feelings and set out our expectations and beliefs as a family without living through it. I believe that if Greg became a slap cam victim, we would already have an understanding of our reaction to the phenomenon and how we would handle the situation. I believe that Greg would know he could come to us. If he was the offender—whether he did the slapping, videotaping, or sharing—then he would know for certain that there would be real consequences to his actions because we had discussed it ahead of time.

Note: I brought up slap camming again when Adam was around, so he could share his thoughts with us. I was delighted that he was as disgusted and confused by it as I was and wasn't going to brush it off as "a guy thing."

What You Should Know about Cyberbullying

○ Your child needs you to be a person they can come to when something online—big or small—doesn't feel right. Keep that door wide open!

○ Initiate conversations about the online world. Keep the discussions casual and comfortable. You might get more information than you imagine when the conversation is two-way. Ask for their opinions. Ask them if they've heard about or seen something that bothers you, tell them what you've read and what you don't understand about it.

○ Share a story about a time you were picked on. They have probably experienced something too—this might be a gateway to sharing uncomfortable life details with one another.

○ Ask your child what it might feel like to be a victim of cyberbullying—to be chronically targeted or picked on. Ask what it might feel like to experience harassment every day, not just a few times, as you grow up. Encourage empathy! These conversations may prevent your child from participating in mean or bullying behavior in the future.

○ Even if the cyberbullying happens on devices at home, it is probably being carried over from problems at school or being brought back into the school environment. It will impact learning and attention!

○ Most school districts have staff trained to deal with cyberbullying. If you are in need of support, your district should have a point of contact for locating resources or advice on cyberbullying.

○ Local law enforcement is also a source of guidance and resources. It is rare to see a juvenile prosecuted for online harassment or cyberbullying. Community-oriented police departments want to work with schools and families to prevent cyberbullying or find a solution before it escalates into a crime.

Cyberbullying is a developing issue. The policies and laws of schools, school districts, and states vary on how they deal with it. There are many variables, but the most crucial point is that we need to be a resource for our children. And our family values need to be strong, then reinforced, in order to teach and practice positive online behaviors.

Report! Block! Delete!

A first step for every child is to report any concerns about online activities to their parents. Delete, hide, or block any of those "friends" who aren't treating you right long before anything becomes harassment—no one deserves it! Facebook has a permanent block option when negative behaviors are reported. Major cell carriers like Sprint and Verizon have an option that lets you block numbers for up to ninety days. Then, if the behaviors resume after the number is unblocked, the carriers encourage victims to report these behaviors to authorities. When in doubt, get some help!

Pay Attention!

I remember being in seventh grade and getting an anonymous letter from a peer that was so mean. It said that my ears stick out, my nose is big, no one likes me, I wore my hair in a ponytail too often, I liked too many different boys, and more. I still remember the color of the paper, the handwriting, the large manila envelope, paragraph upon paragraph of lashing out. It stung. I remember lying down on my bed and curling up with the letter nearby, my spirit a little broken. But what I remember best, the most lasting impact of this entire experience, is when my mother came into my room to put away some clean clothes. She noticed something wasn't right. She sat on the side of my bed and asked me what was wrong. I didn't want her to think that I wasn't okay or that someone might not like me, so I continued to say that nothing was wrong, I was just tired. She stayed there, sitting quietly. After a few silent minutes, I handed her the letter and she read it. She gave me a hug. I cried it out. We talked about it. She helped me process and understand that people who are hurt sometimes want to hurt other people. We talked about what qualities good friends have. My mom was mad and hurt too. She helped me move on. See, she was in tune with me, with my behaviors, and guided me to better understand my peers and their motivations. She noticed! As parents we may not have the perfect words or solutions, but we have to pay attention.

Just like my mom was in tune with me, you can be in tune with your kids too! It is especially important that we do frequent check-ins because of the challenges posed and the isolation imposed by cyber-bullying. Even though it often happens in our very own homes, we might never see it! But we might see some behaviors that come with it. The NCPC shares some classic symptoms of cyberbullying on its Web site. Some of them are:

○ Your child doesn't want to do activities that they are usually inter-ested in.
○ There are changes in sleeping or eating habits.
○ Your child shutting down the computer or hiding the screen when someone comes near could mean they're cyberbullying someone.
○ Your child using the computer or cell phone excessively might also mean they're cyberbullying.
○ There's a change in who's in your child's circle of friends.
○ Your child starts getting in trouble at school.

Cyberbullying is preventable. Parents must talk to their children about it, ask them what they have seen, help them identify it, and encourage them to express their online challenges, problems, and conflicts with you. Even if they fear losing their technology use privi-leges, it should not be kept a secret!

Friend Fail

Julie wakes up at a friend's house after a group sleepover. Just as she opens her eyes, tired and groggy from getting hardly any sleep, Katie snaps a photo. The photo is posted and public within seconds, before Julie can even react. Katie professes that she was "just kidding," that sharing the pic online wasn't meant maliciously and is "no big deal." Meanwhile, dozens of male and female peers see it and comment on, repost, and share the photo. Embarrassed, Julie begs Katie to take the photo down, and even though Katie does, it has already appeared in too many places to be removed permanently. This is a friend fail. Katie hurt and humiliated her, and once Katie realized this, it was too late. The difference between a friend fail and cyberbullying is that a friend fail is not chronic or threatening, but rather unkind or unfair treatment by a friend who has the same level of social power.

Permission to Post! is a strategy I teach as a reminder to kids, teens, and adults to seek approval before tagging, posting, or sharing pictures of another person. This simple courtesy might be extended in a meaningful (no matter how brief) conversation that looks like this.

Katie: Hey Julie, can I post that funny pic of you waking up to Instagram?

Julie: Let me see. No, I look horrible! But you can send it to Jenny because she'll crack up at my tired eyes.

Gregory and his friends were taking pictures of each other dunking on a friend's adjustable basketball hoop in our neighborhood. When they got a shot they liked and had edited it to make each other look pretty awesome (hang time, swag, dunk style, facial expressions), they posted them on Instagram. Later that night I was scrolling through Greg's pics and noticed that he had posted a few unflattering pictures of one of their buddies, Joey, trying to get the right dunk and had added a few sarcastic captions. It bothered me enough to ask

Greg about it, and I had a good feeling we were headed in the direction of having a very teachable moment. I felt like Greg and his friends
were trying to build themselves up or make themselves look better by
putting down or making fun of another friend.

> **Me:** Hey, why do you, Scott, and Tyler look awesome in your
> pics, but only Joey's outtakes got posted?
>
> **Greg:** Because they're funny. It's not a big deal. He doesn't
> care. Mom, Joey thinks they're funny too.
>
> **Me:** Did he say that? Did you ask him if you could post those?
> *(I carry on about the value of remembering to use the Permission
> to Post! strategy.)*
>
> **Greg:** Okay, Mom, but I know he doesn't care.
>
> **Me:** Would you care if those pics were of you?
>
> **Greg:** Probably.
>
> **Me:** So do me a favor and ask Joey if he wants those pictures
> posted. You can leave them if he clears it. Otherwise, be a
> good friend and take them down.

As it turned out, Joey did ask Greg to take them down. He
agreed that it wasn't a huge deal, but said he'd rather not have them
shared. This is a great example of how we can use iRules to encourage our children to be good friends and to consider the feelings of
others— thinking before you act applies to the screens as well. We
need to teach our tech-savvy kids to look out for the best interests of
others, instead of posting something just to score a lot of likes or
attention.

In another scenario I heard about, a group of girls were hanging at
a friend's house in one of the bedrooms. Three of the girls broke out
into a dance, singing into the mirror, being silly and cracking up. Two of
the girls decided to sneak a video of it and immediately posted it to
Vine. The other girls had no idea it'd been posted until they opened

their accounts later that night. Then they found out it had gotten more than a hundred favorites and thirty-some comments.

This story illustrates what I fear our children are losing the most—all opportunity to be "off." Our tweens and teens are feeling the pressure to always be on, engaged, and looking their best because pictures can be sent and shared instantly. They are constantly aware of what they're doing, who they are with, and how they look. Children need a consistent safe zone where they can let down their guard and not worry about their appearance—a place where they can just be themselves. Our teens and children need strategies they can use to navigate the technology together, with being a good friend and a good person as their first priority. I believe that we can preserve this for our children. We have the power to protect them against the full invasion of technology. It doesn't belong in every nook and cranny of their lives.

The Power of Language

Scroll through your child's Instagram or Twitter account and I promise that you'll find words like "gay," "slut," and "pimp" littered throughout the comments. According to the Twitter Tracker at ThinkB4YouSpeak.com, the word "fag" is typically used more than a million times every month. These words are used casually, in jest, or without thought. "That's not what I meant. We're just kidding around" is something I've heard from teens time and again on this topic. So I ask them to describe what they *actually* meant. What usually follows are words like "weird," "dumb," "cool," or "different." Language is a powerful tool that can impact people even when that isn't the speaker's intention. But words do have consequences! Many of these words constitute hate language and have no place being tossed around virtually or in reality. Whenever I see or hear kids and teens using this language, instead of scolding them or embarrassing them, I simply say, "Find a different word." This little phrase is something that catches on. I hear them repeat it to each other, so I know I have alerted them to be aware of language, while also encouraging them to say exactly what they mean and not hide behind words that can be hurtful or offensive to others.

When I lead parenting workshops, I ask parents to tell me how they prepare their children for specific tech use. One woman wanted her son to know that most parents scroll through texts, online accounts, and all histories, so he should assume that every person he communicates with would also have to show their parents the content and details of their phones. She told him not to use language another parent wouldn't like to see. In other words, if you wouldn't say it, don't type it. This perspective helped her son see her point clearly: Do you want your friend's parent to read what you wrote?

Parent to Parent

One of the most common questions—posed in many different ways—that I am asked in my parent coaching sessions is whether to tell another child's parent when that child posts something of concern. There need to be some baseline questions you ask yourself before taking any action.

○   Does the comment, picture, status, or conversation reveal something dangerous, life threatening, or against the law? If the answer is yes and speaking to Judy will protect her daughter from harm, then please have a parent conversation immediately. Even if Judy doesn't like what you have to say, ultimately, you need to put your head on the pillow at night and know you didn't keep quiet.

○   If you do not believe the situation to be dangerous, then ask yourself these questions: *What is my relationship with Judy like? How would I react if Judy came to me with the same information about my child? Can Judy handle this conversation with maturity or will she feel judged or attacked? What do I hope to accomplish by bringing this to Judy's attention? Are my reasons genuine, or am I being melodramatic?*

If Judy is a close and open friend, hopefully you will have established some boundaries about such matters prior to an occurrence taking place. My mother-in-law, Karen, raised four boys. Her two closest friends were also raising sons that were the same ages, and all of the boys were close friends. When the boys became teenagers, the mothers had an agreement that they would report to each other on the others' sons only if a hospital, jail, or serious bloodshed were involved. This agreement also included anything that might be embarrassing or damaging to the family or hard to hear from someone else. This had a profound and long-lasting impact on the friendship because they set ground rules from the beginning and everyone stood by those expectations. Other friendships might work best when everything is shared in a safe and understanding relationship. If Judy is a close girlfriend, saying "I saw a picture of Julie drinking a beer on Instagram" might feel safe and comfortable. Again, only you can assess each relationship and start from there.

If Judy is not a close friend or is someone you hardly know and the situation is not dangerous or life threatening, pause before telling her. Judy has some obligation to be present online for her children and will probably (hopefully!) make her way there eventually. And there's a chance that she's already seen it, or behaviors like it, anyway. The reality is, we are only in control of our own families and our own households.

And don't forget that the online behaviors we see from others present teachable moments for our own children. They allow us to open the door and talk about different scenarios before our children are actually involved in anything similar. This dialogue can be crucial for developing healthy tech relationships because we are not talking about potential dangers or what-ifs and can walk our children through an actual situation.

So What Are Kids Talking about Online?

I think almost all tweens and teens are talking about their interests. I see them talking about games, school productions, professional sports teams, inspiring or funny quotes, celebrities, school, music, food, fashion, family, parties, peers, vacations, the weather, and other interests. Most days what I read is pretty standard. We can gain real understanding of who our children are and what they are into by looking at their online profiles and updates. (I think this is true for us adults too! Think of your own Facebook page—it probably represents you and what you're into pretty well!) There are so many clues available online—what's happening in their relationships, what music they love, trends, disappointments, what they're excited about, and what changes are occurring. We can use their online presence to gain insight into who our children are, how they portray themselves, and how they relate to and interact with their peers. It's not always great that our children share so much online, but we don't need to look too hard to get a sense of what's happening in their day-to-day (often, hour-to-hour) lives.

Parent Tip: *Look to see if your child's online personality matches their real-life personality. Do the interests match? Do their tone of voice, energy, and spirit sound the same when they post and share online with their peers? We want to make sure that the relationship with technology is healthy. Encourage your kids to be authentic in the real and virtual worlds!*

As discussed before, seeing our children's friends post or comment online provides a great opportunity to deepen the dialogue with our own children. What follows are some sample conversations to have about peer behavior online. *It is really important to act like you "get it" when talking to your kids.* The more shocked, outraged, or critical we are of our children's peers, the more closed off from us they'll be. The more we act like we can handle it (even if we are in fact outraged), the more likely it is that our kids will come to us again to present questions and concerns in the future.

These are actual conversations that I've had with Gregory and Brendan. Each time a conversation followed the observations.

O   I noticed that Sam's recent tweets were all referencing pot. I asked Greg, "Did you see that? What's up with that? Do you think he's into it?" Greg opened up to me about some of the kids he knows trying pot.

O   Kimmy was always so harsh about herself online, saying she's fat or ugly. This led us to have a brief discussion about girls posting online to get attention or positive feedback, like "You're not fat! You're beautiful! You're perfect!"

O   JP's Instagram has all serious selfies. I said, "Is that the image he's going for? What I love most about him is his sweet and funny nature. Why all the swag online?" We talked about how some people create false online personalities and the motivation behind it.

Build a Community!

When we have a set of iRules to guide us, our conversations with our children become more deliberate and clearer. We can reference a point within our own agreement openly and honestly with our children. Parents should not feel isolated or alone in parenting technology. An iRules agreement will take the struggle out of it and encourage dialogue and cooperation instead.

When our children were young, we sat together during story hour at the library or chatted with them while we pushed them on the swings in the park. We set up playgroups and had coffee with other parents. We read books and online articles, and went to workshops and discussed time-outs, toilet training, teething, and feedings. Soon our kids started school, and activities and homework now take up most weekdays. We are carpooling and shuffling around every day. Somewhere in this transition, we stop deliberately talking to each other about raising children. The developmental milestones become less important, and we often deal with the struggles and challenges of raising teens and tweens on our own. Stop this! Make a big kids' play-group that meets weekly—once a month, even—after school or after work and let the kids run around on the playground together while you connect with other parents. Set up a coffee hour at your local library for those who are parenting teens. No one needs to be an expert to share with and support each other.

The most amazing experiences I have in the workshops I lead happen during what I call "the softening," when relief comes over the faces of parents about midway through the session. Everyone comes through the door overwhelmed by the idea of a parenting technology workshop. Should they share their story about their son's mistakes? Should they admit to not knowing anything about Twitter? And then we get going. We start sharing, and guess what? They find out that a few different people have had similar experiences when someone asks the question they thought would make them seem like a slacker par-ent. And then they don't feel so alone anymore. We've built a safe place to be flawed, to ask questions, to not know, to seek support. And that's a beautiful thing!

I always start by telling attendees, "Who wants to sign up for a healthy-eating class when you've been hitting the drive-thru every night?" No one! Families are constantly bombarded by what they "should" be doing, but I want them to know that parenting technol-ogy is not daunting, it's possible. I don't want the workshop (or this book) to overwhelm anyone. I want it to empower them. The best way to empower is to offer resources and support for people to lean on and to share with others. That builds community. It really does take a village. Use yours!

To build my personal village and connect within my community, I had to take responsibility for making relationships happen. How do you begin doing this? The most beautiful and direct way for me to answer such a question is to tell you to leave your phone behind. Go on, head out into the world—go to that PTA family event, that library story time, the playground, the soccer field, the church fund-raiser—phone-free. Volunteer for a community activity—coach, teach, plan, build, make, take direction. Introduce yourself. Catch up with someone you've met before. Let the kids show you the way. If they make a buddy, say, "Show me who your parents are" and go say hello (kids are great buffers in all things uncomfortable).

When we moved to Cape Cod, I had three kids under five years old. At first I knew how to get to the grocery store, the library, and around my neighborhood. That's it. So that's all I did—over and over—until that became my community. I met the librarian, who introduced me to the other librarians, who introduced me to families that were frequent patrons of the library. Then those families told me about free story times and community playgroups and family social clubs and activities. And my village expanded.

Start a conversation with someone new during a youth sporting event or music lesson, talk about things you have in common—like parenting or a book you like. Go for a walk or a cup of coffee with an acquaintance. Don't worry about checking your e-mail, snapping a great photo, or what's happening on Facebook, just try building a new personal connection or two every time you are out. Soon your village will expand. Soon your conversations will become more meaningful, more deliberate. Ask questions like "What video games do your kids like?" "What boundaries do you set?" and "Does your daughter have a cell phone? How do you manage her use of it?" It is important to build relationships for parenting topics like technology so we feel we have resources, for opportunities to explore thoughts and ideas, and so we never feel alone. I have learned so much from other parents', families', and community members' experiences and beliefs. And even though our methods or opinions are often different, we still gain so much insight into our own parenting styles and beliefs when we raise our families connected in community.

And talk about community! After our iRules contract went viral, everyone in town had their eyes on Greg's cell use. And he knew it. We laughed about it a lot. People would see him at the gym or after school and say, "Hoff—you doing what your mother said?" A few parent friends said to me over the month after Christmas, "Janell, he's really following your contract!" Even his good buddy agreed: "Janell, you know that Greg's not breaking your rules, right? I mean, I like your contract and everything, I just hope you don't see my mom anytime soon. She has no idea how much I use my phone." And I loved how kids and adults were giving us feedback and checking in on us. Communities are so important to help us look out for and support our children. Recently the owner of a local coffee shop said to me, "Janell, I was really happy to see that Greg's appetite doesn't seem to be affected by his concussion. He had a huge lunch when he came in yesterday." That's my community! And I'm so much better because of it.

🗹 **iRule Tip:** Have the same behavioral standards for your child online that you do offline. Use your family values to parent technology. It's that easy. If you do not want your child to use certain language or call someone names, do not allow it on the screen either. If you teach your child to be kind to others and to avoid lying and being deceitful, you should apply those same beliefs to the technology.

PART 2

Responsibility

Say "please" and "thank you," make eye contact, work hard, value what you have, bask in gratitude, honor your family, set high standards, engage, exercise, think.

○ ● ○

Manners Matter

iRule: Manners

> **My iRule:** If it rings, answer it. It is a phone. Say hello, use your manners. Do not ever ignore a phone call if the screen reads "Mom" or "Dad." Not ever.

Why do manners matter? Why dwell on politeness? Does it seem archaic to dedicate an entire chapter to manners when we're talking about modern parenting and technology? Our cultural expectations on manners have certainly softened over the years. Children can wiggle in their seats and eat with their fingers more than ever before. Today we ask our kids questions like "What do you want for dinner?" "Where should we spend the day today?" and "When do you want to leave?" When I was about four years old, my mother bought me a shirt that read KIDS ARE PEOPLE, TOO! That idea, in the early '80s, was new! To think that kids had thoughts and feelings and opinions and rights was an actual movement, and a television program too. My mom and I talk about that shirt all the time. She was proud to be making a statement that her little girl should be *seen* and *heard*. And I was! In a way that went like this: She asked what part of *Charlotte's Web*—or math class, or a field trip—was my favorite, and whether I wanted to try out for the softball team, take flute lessons, go to college, I had a say. I contributed opinions that were respected and often considered by adults. And my mother, who grew up in the '60s and '70s with three brothers and conventionally thinking parents, called that progress. Because children being "seen and not heard" was slowly becoming an idea of the past. But after parenting young children for fourteen years, I firmly believe we should carry some of that long-ago thinking in our back pockets to sprinkle on our families as needed. The idea of having respect for oneself, for others, for elders, for other young people should be at the center of what we teach. It is not about having power over children, it is about raising them to understand how to have respect for all.

During the media frenzy over my original iRules contract, I was asked boatloads of questions about my parenting style. Everyone wanted to label me, put me into a category. When I talked about "assessing my child's maturity" and "following the child" before making decisions, I was deemed permissive or attached. When I talked about "setting boundaries" and "leading my children," I was called old-fashioned and authoritarian. I am none of these and all of these and more. I see a little bit of myself, of my parenting struggles, successes, and styles, in everyone. However, this does not make a great answer in a national news interview. It's too vague and too boring. It's too true. There is no story or headline to stick on me. During one interview I was asked, "So, you let your kids make the rules for themselves?" *No.* "You believe children and adults are on the same level of the hierarchy?" *No.* There is a chain of command, and Adam and I are at the top. This is important to remember as we build family iRules. That doesn't mean we don't have conversations or discuss ideas. We do want our children to feel heard. After all, kids are people too! We want them to take ownership of their tech boundaries and guidelines, but ultimately we decide. When we direct the ship, the steering becomes much easier.

But in some ways, today the scale has tipped to the side opposite to that of forty or so years ago. Kids' needs are now everything! Our expectations for and beliefs about our children have shifted. Now the convention is that they should always be comfortable—physically and emotionally. They should be happy, with their needs met, bellies full, attention engaged, workloads easily manageable. They should be achieving—busy, studying, and participating in extracurricular activities that we pay for. And I do this too! By design, I have put my children smack-dab in the center of my world. Everything we do and do not do is rooted in the "impact" it will have on or the "value" it will have for our household—more specifically, for the children. But still, it tugs at me. We make our lives revolve—*literally*—around the needs of our children. And that's good, right? *But is it?* Shouldn't they revolve around us in some ways too? I mean, if I'm going to put my feet on the floor every morning to feed, water, love, drive, help, and grow these little cherubs, why can't I have really high expectations of them in return? I can be intense, I expect a lot from people—I really do. But it feels vital to hold our children to especially high standards on how they treat people. That's right, *people* like us—their parents! At the very basic level, the one way they can return all this giving and doing and sacrificing is to look us in the eye and say "please" and "thank you"—even over the technology!

The most confident and respected teens and young adults I meet, supervise, and work with are well-mannered. Last summer I worked with a quiet and kind high school student, Michael, who said "good morning," "please," "thank you," "excuse me," with such ease and consistency that even his peers couldn't help but compliment him. It was

iPhone Manners Fail (Almost)
A Gentle Reminder That Using Good Manners (Even in a Text Convo) Goes a Long Way

It's Saturday, 8:30 a.m.; my phone chimes that there's an incoming text from Greg, who spent the night at his friend's house.

Greg: When are you coming?

Janell: Good morning, Greg. How are you today?

Greg: Hi. I'm ready to go. I had a terrible night's sleep. I want to be picked up before 10:00.

Janell: Well, I'm at work. I know you're cranky, but you can't be rude. You'll need to find a nicer way to ask.

Greg: Mom, could you please pick me up as soon as possible? I didn't sleep great and I'd love to get a nap in before my game. Thank you.

Janell: Much better! Let me finish up a few things and I'll hustle over to get you!

Janell: PS—See how well that works? ☺

Greg: Yesssss, Mom. ☺

a reminder to me both to continue to stress the importance of good manners to my children and to use those same good manners myself. When I asked Michael about it, he told me that the adults at his high school taught students to greet people by saying hello and addressing them by name. He said that he felt it was important to greet people with eye contact and a warm smile or exchange. Because he was taught this by people he respected, it carried over into every part of his life and became a habit.

I volunteer in Cassidy's preschool classroom, and one day a poster caught my eye. It read: BE KIND, RESPECTFUL, HELPFUL, POLITE, A FRIEND. They strike me, these powerful words. We are teaching our youngest children these very basic but important manners. It's comfortable to teach a four-year-old to be polite—to give a smile, a thank-you. It feels natural. But our thirteen-year-olds, for whom the world often feels awkward—how can we be certain they maintain such standards? How do we make clear our expectations? We need to nurture these qualities as they grow by practicing using good manners all the time, so it's second nature, like it is to Michael. We need to have high expectations for our children, to believe that they really are capable and intuitive enough to offer to give up their seats, to open a door for someone. I do not believe that teenagers can hide behind the idea that they are known to be moody, cranky, and disrespectful. I would love to have the cultural standard reset so we would not be surprised when a group of teenagers walking past us said hello and smiled. I remember when my children were very young, I stopped in the grocery store to talk to a neighbor that had four of her children shopping with her. They probably ranged from ten to sixteen years old then. I remember we talked for twenty minutes or so in the aisle. Her children stood by politely, letting their mother talk. As we carried on, there wasn't an eye roll or disgruntled look or action from any of them. I remember seeing her soon after and asking, "How did you get all of your children to be so polite?" She said it was all about the expectations she set for them. That really stuck with me. Our children will meet us where our expectations are. If we allow them to pull, beg, whine, interrupt (I'm not talking so much about toddlers here), then they will. If we believe and enforce an expectation that they will stand by quietly while adults speak, say "please" and "thank you," offer someone a seat, lend a hand, then they will.

Slow Tech Communication Practice

If you need to have a personal conversation—a friend wants to talk about her divorce or her child's concussion, or your mom wants to tell you about Aunt Judy's surgery or her neighbor's dog dying—wait. Just stop. Do not have this conversation while driving for the carpool or running errands. Make the time to sit somewhere quiet and chat—over the phone or in person. I see so many women trying to be good friends and daughters, but only half listening to intimate details of the life of someone they care about while grabbing cereal off the grocery store shelf or picking the kids up at school. It just doesn't work! It's rude to all parties involved, and even though you think you're saving time, you're failing yourself, the people you are with (most likely your kids), the people in public that can see and hear you trying to have a life talk, and the person on the other end of the phone, because you're not present anywhere! So stop! Wait. Make the time and give this conversation your full attention.

Anticipate and plan for how long a conversation might take. Do not start a conversation that you really want to sink your teeth into at 3:50 if you need to pick up your child at school at 4:00. This won't work. And you know it! I used to be the queen of this. I would finally get twelve minutes alone when I was driving to a doctor's appointment, and I would want to call everyone

I believe this is true about technology behaviors too. We can expect our children to use manners and be respectful while using technology. It does not have to be a common occurrence that we roll our eyes and say "Teenagers!" as if they are excused from being civil

I'd been missing or meaning to catch. Then I would reach them and dig into the conversation for about eight minutes and then start to panic. I'd have one emotional foot in the conversation and one physical foot out of the car, knowing I needed to hustle inside. These were stressful times because I'd end up being late for my appointment or cutting off the person I was talking to. Now I try to preserve my energy a little more. I take these moments of aloneness in the car and listen to music or grab an iced coffee and enjoy it while driving. That's it. But it's still not easy to keep myself from calling.

There is that slight chance when you're a busy, social parent that if you follow these Slow Tech prompts, it may never be a good time to call a friend or listen intently to your own mother talk about her day. So schedule it! Just like you would schedule a class at the gym or a dentist appointment. Once a week, I try to call one friend and chat for twenty to thirty minutes. I sometimes do this while folding sky-high piles of laundry, driving into the city, while the kids are watching television or bike riding in the neighborhood. I will often text my mom and say, "Let's chat tomorrow afternoon when you get out of work. I can't wait to catch up." Then it's a date!

because of their developmental stage. We can set high standards for online behaviors and get results from our children. Raising children now includes raising them on the technology.

We all know what an impact good manners can have. We have all met and interacted with a teen or child that shakes our hand, that says "hello" with eye contact and "please" and "thank you" with ease. We remember these children. I could make a quick list of ten teens right now that have left me thinking, *I really like that kid. He is so polite.* I don't lump them in with whatever group they were part of—the team, the camp kids, school friends—they stand out on their own. I can remember this as a child too. My mother would commonly say, "I love polite kids." She drew attention to them, used them as models to show us what it looked like and felt like to be treated and to treat others with such obvious respect. This helped shape how I wanted other parents to think of me. I believe that manners—including virtual manners—send a message.

Technology has made much of our communication informal. And because of that, we can be casual and curt with each other in text messages in a way we wouldn't be over the phone or in person. Take a scroll through your own texts. Are you starting conversations with "Hello, [name], how are you? Is this a good time to chat?" I know I'm not. I really try to be aware of the time of day when I'm texting so as not to wake sleeping people, but still, whenever I have a thought or idea, I usually just text it then. I find it a real struggle to wait until the next day at work or when I see that person again to tell them a story, my thoughts, or something funny. In the book *Teen Manners,* written by Cindy Post Senning and Peggy Post, it says, "What times are okay for calling? A good guide is no earlier than nine in the morning and no later than nine at night." I love applying this clear boundary not just to calling, but to texting, FaceTime and Skype sessions, and other person-to-person online interactions. If I take a look through texts I've sent to my co-workers, there are loads of scattered messages: "Can you do this?" "Did you see that?" "What is your take on that?" "Who will be here then?" And of course, with the people I am closest to, I can be totally rude!

Even if I'm being not rude but concise, a lot of meaning can be lost from the dialogue. If text messaging becomes our primary way to communicate, we'll have to look at that gap. It's easy to say that my point was conveyed, noted, understood, and acted upon in much less time than a wordier message would have been. And we don't want to carry on and on in texts, but what is missing? How aren't we relating to people? How deliberately are we communicating? The Slow Tech movement holds that a phone call allows for a more meaningful give-and-take conversation. That kind of interaction is still important! Believe me, I use (overuse!) text messaging every day. I love it. It might be my favorite part of technology (besides GPS) because it saves time, it keeps people connected, and it's just so easy. But I really feel that we all need to be aware and to mindfully communicate, even if it's over text messaging. We also need to teach those principles to our children, because quick, convenient communication is all they really know. How can we be sure to help preserve high-quality interaction? How can we be sure we're texting what we really want to say?

Please Pause for Other Parents

A mother came to me genuinely concerned by the fact that the morning after she hosted a sleepover for a group of her daughter's friends, the girls just left. Mothers texted daughters upon arriving at the driveway and daughters slipped out of the house with a quick good-bye. The mother said to me, "Janell, these are women I have known for years. We raised our girls together. And now, because all of the kids have cell phones, we don't even communicate anymore. We don't check in. We don't go to the door to collect our kids and say thank you. We don't ask questions like 'Did everything go okay?' Parents have stopped talking to each other. It worries me. I just feel really bothered that phones are making adults rude. Doesn't it seem natural to want to come in and check in with a parent at the home where your twelve-year-old just spent the night? What are we doing? I mean, some of the girls were picked up and I didn't even know it."

These are times when I wonder what the trade-off is for the convenience of technology. Are we getting lazier? Busier? Disconnected? It does seem easy to text Gregory at a sleepover and say, "Picking up at 10am, be ready to go." And I have done that. But I have always tried to at least connect with the adult involved to express my gratitude, to make sure Greg behaved, to say hello. I was actually thrilled to hear another mother express her unhappiness about this new consequence of teen tech culture. It's such a great perspective, one worthy of real discussion.

If you are picking up your child at a friend's house, get off your phone, walk up to the house, and say thank you to the person that hosted them. Even if you have to get somewhere else right away, make a real attempt to go inside and thank the family. If you do not have time to chat in person, make a phone call prior to leaving your house that sounds like this: "Hi, Betty, I'm leaving in about five minutes to get Allie. I'll be rushing her to practice before I head to work, so I just wanted to say thanks for having her over last night." Let's preserve our relationships with our children's peers' families. Even if "relationship" means simply saying thank you. That is all.

What about the Kids?

So my mother used to wrap herself up in the kitchen phone cord and talk to her girlfriends or my grandmother for hours (probably minutes, but at age seven, it was really an eternity). I don't really know what they talked about, but a five-minute "We're on our way" call would often turn into a much longer discussion on why marriage is a challenge or real estate prices. When I was a teenager, I too sat behind a closed door and talked for hours on our landline to friends and boyfriends about details, homework, sports, plans, funny things, and pure foolishness. We were a house of talkers. I don't think that my mother was consciously allowing me space to have meaningful dialogue with peers so I could live a life of purpose. I don't really think she was thinking about it all that much.*

---

*Except on the nights when I talked too long and my homework wasn't done, then she would really care. Then she would yell up the stairs, "Time's up!" And then she would pick up the other extension and say, "Get off the phone." And then she would tell my dad. And then (I can only remember this happening one time) he would walk into my bedroom without speaking and pull the phone cord right out of the wall—phone jack and all. Time is up.

First of all, she could hear me. She could figure out what I was talking about based on my end of the conversation. If she wanted details, she just had to stroll past my door and listen. Second, I was attached to a three-foot cord, curled up in a hoodie against the wall near my bed. I could only stay there so long. She knew that soon I'd come running to meet those people and go to those places and execute those plans. The phone could not come with me! *Not to the car, not to the mall, not to my friend's house, not playing ball.* See, there was a limit to what I could do with a phone, and so there was an end. But now there is not.

It seems that no place is sacred; the technology and social communication creep in everywhere. So we have to try—really make an effort—to preserve the "end." We must make sure that our children walk through parts of their lives without talking, texting, chatting, scrolling. It's not that we can't be talkers anymore—I know I celebrate the social ease provided by technology—it's that we have to make sure our kids uncurl from the corners of their bedrooms, get up, and go do.

Who Are You Hanging With?

One comment I hear from parents over and again is that they do not know everyone that their kids are connecting with online. And since they hardly know the peers, they certainly don't know the parents. My mother was the queen of this core philosophy whenever I left my house to go to someone else's: She had to know whether the parents were going to be home, and if she didn't know them, then she had to meet them before I was allowed to stay. I will never forget one night when I was in seventh grade; I had been invited to hang out with a group of young high school boys and girls that I had become friendly with.

Note: *It was actually Adam's group of friends, and that was the night I first kissed him. Yes, my Adam. But that's a story for another day. Or another book. And damn, was my mother paying attention.*

My mom knew the kids well enough, but did not know the host family. I was mortified that she was going to drop me off with all of these cooler older kids there and say, "Are your parents home?" like I was a little kid. But that didn't stop her, she did it anyway. The father came out and met her, she was reasonably satisfied, and she left me there for two hours. I look back now and see that she was doing a few things by introducing herself. She was saying:

O   My child is here. Know that.
O   I am her mother. Know that.
O   You are responsible for her. Know that.
O   Thank you for opening your home to her. I appreciate that.

I think that modern parents are thirsty for even these small conversations and introductions. If you want to know whom your children are hanging out with, if you want to know their families, find a way. If you want to meet eyeballs-to-eyeballs, then require it.

iRule Tip: One of the major reasons I purchased this technology for my son was to increase the convenience of our communication. So he needs to answer the phone! Why did you purchase the technology in your home and what are your firm expectations for the use of that purchase? Identify them and apply them!

iRule: Etiquette

> **My iRule:** Turn it off, silence it, put it away in public. Especially in a restaurant, at the movies, or while speaking with another human being. You are not a rude person; do not allow the iPhone to change that.

Etiquette is defined by the Merriam-Webster online dictionary as "the conduct or procedure required by good breeding or prescribed by authority to be observed in social or official life." The "good breeding" portion of this definition jumps out at me. It immediately makes me think of child rearing and parenthood. It reminds me that our job requires that we teach our children etiquette in all of its forms. I think about my own dinner table. Dinnertime can be dicey. I would not feel confident heading to dinner at the White House or Buckingham Palace. We give these very basic orders over and again: "Bottom on the chair, feet forward, use your fork, knife, napkin. Stop. Don't shout. Hands to yourself. Chew slowly. Ask nicely. Take turns. Say thank you." I try to imagine what they might do at the dinner table in someone else's home when they're invited to share a meal. It frightens me enough to never give up on insisting that my children reach my expectations.

Recently I was e-mailed a story. A family invited their daughter's eighteen-year-old boyfriend to their home for dinner. It was the first time most of the family had met him. It was a nice offering—an occasion, in the family's eyes. He sat down at the table and, at some point during the meal, he took out his phone and started texting. The family, shooting each other looks of disbelief, let it go. Then he did it again. The family was horrified. The daughter was embarrassed. The father said in disbelief, "If you have more interesting things to say and do on that phone, then why don't you go home and do it." The boyfriend was shocked and surprised. He said he never meant to be rude, he was just checking something. They asked him to please put his phone away for the remainder of the evening. The mother told me she wanted to kick him out, but truly believed he hadn't seen anything wrong with his behavior. He'd had no idea, no education about family and technology etiquette. I felt for this family. I felt for the young man too. That was his chance to make a first impression, and it was one that the family will never forget.

Teaching tech etiquette is new to the parenting list of things to do. But it is imperative because whether we like it or not, it speaks volumes about our children. I feel strongly that every child and teenager, even in the face of the greatest temptation, must resist the urge to use their personal technology while visiting someone's home or meeting someone for the first time. Otherwise, I believe, it says "disinterested," "bored," or "rude," when they may not feel that at all. We have all the time in the world to scroll and tweet and text; save it for personal time away from the dinner table in someone else's home.

So much of what our children (and we) do is about habit. Do you pick up your phone and scroll for no reason? I do. Do you reach for your phone every time you leave the car or leave a building or meeting? I do. Through working on this book, I have started to pay very close attention to my tech habits and their relationship to tech etiquette. I have imagined how intense the urge to check, scroll, and text must be for our children. How can we help them control it and make sure that their tech habits are in accord with our family expectations? When we shine a light on their habits, it becomes clear to them. Gentle reminders like "Why don't you hang out with your buddies while they are here, you can check your phone when they leave," and "Girls, why don't you try for a selfie-free hour before we need to drive to practice?"

Non-Tech House Rules

Think about the ways your home is run like a series of agreements in matters unrelated to technology. We enforce rules in our homes all the time. Here are some household agreements unrelated to technology that are understood and practiced every day, shared with me by my blog readers.

○ Whoever sets the dinner table doesn't have to help clear it.
○ Offer an adult your chair.
○ Sundays are family days—no birthday parties, no playdates, no meetings.
○ No one can play football until fifth grade.
○ We split the cost of sneakers.
○ Lunches must be made the night before.
○ Homework must be done before going outside to play.
○ No back-to-back sleepovers.

help kids recognize their behaviors, as opposed to sweeping generalizations like "You're always on your phone!"

If this doesn't work or the kids don't follow your prompts, enforce a house rule for all peers when they visit. I know a local family that collects all the guests' cell phones at 9:00 p.m. during sleepovers. The parents explain to the visiting children that it's their "house iRule" that all the kids follow, including those that are visiting. We have told our kids' friends, "No phones at the dinner table" and "Please don't take pictures or videos of Greg's younger siblings and post or share them—

- No clean laundry should find its way into the hamper.
- At cookouts and parties, one soda per event.
- No friends of the opposite gender in your bedroom.

These family agreements give a baseline for behaviors. These house rules are not fought about or even discussed daily, they're just agreements understood within families. iRules work the same way. iRules are a set of agreements about technology use built on family understanding, values, and needs. The great thing about a set of iRules is that our kids can see it as routine family life, because we've laid it out so clearly. And because we've weaved iRules into our lives, they can be used just like our other house rules. "I can't go on that Web site" works just like "Sorry, I can't come to your house today, because every Sunday is family day."

even if they're of something cute." I recently connected with a Texas mother of several teenagers that said she's being so clear with her tech limits that as soon as her teens' peers enter her house, she says, "We don't take pictures and share them here, we turn off phones at 10:00, we only talk online to people we would talk to in person. Do you think you can do that?" Sometimes speaking up and setting boundaries can be uncomfortable for us, for our children, and for the visiting children. But it is important that we hold true to our own values or behaviors In varied circumstances. This is also designed to protect the visiting children from getting into trouble while you are responsible for them and teaches them to adapt to other parenting styles and tech comfort levels. Kids that genuinely like your children will stick around no matter what your rules are. Kids that can't agree to your house iRules temporarily? Well, they probably shouldn't be visiting anyway.

Below I have related a set of real situations that my readers have observed, each accompanied by tangible strategies we can apply to remedy them.

The Violation Station

Violation: Ordering or having any kind of service performed for you while talking on the phone.

Solution: Say to the person you're talking to, "Can I call you right back? I'm about to get an oil change [or order a sandwich, ask for directions, buy a pack of gum]."

Violation: Crossing the street or walking in a public place with your gaze focused on the device.

Solution: Put the phone in your pocket while you're walking. Or stop and sit on a bench to text, search, and scroll the day away.

Violation: Having a long, loud phone conversation in public. (Eek! Too many details!)

Solution: Say, "Hey, I'm on a bus [or in a store, eating pizza, surrounded by strangers]—let's catch up later."

Violation: Chronically or obsessively checking your phone while you're hanging with actual people.

Solution: Have a conversation with the people you can see and touch. Turn your phone off or activate the DO NOT DISTURB setting. Make this a priority: Value real time.

Violation: Saying "Wait. Hold on. Wait. Hold on" to our children while we are distracted by our devices.*

Solution: Set concrete, nonnegotiable times to check your phone, e-mail, read a great article, watch a YouTube video throughout the day. These breaks will allow you guilt-free time to catch up and enjoy the technology. At all other times, put down your phone and be present with your child. Create personal boundaries.

---

*I had to include this violation, because I am so guilty of it. Must. Stop. Checking. Phone.

Violation (Challenge): An old friend calls unexpectedly and you are excited! Even though you are about to go into the market, you answer the call anyway. Your friend starts right into a personal story of heartbreak or difficulty and cannot be stopped. Your time is limited. You need to get this errand done. But you don't want to hurt her feelings. You try to shop and listen.

Solution: If you decide to answer a call in public or when you are in a hurry, preface the conversation by setting a boundary like "It is so great to hear from you! I have ten minutes before I have to go into the store. Do you want to talk now or catch up later when I have more time?"

If you decide that the call is important enough to make you skip your errand or be late for an appointment, then make it the priority. Stay in your car or find somewhere private to give this friend your full attention. Do not try to do both.

Observation Station

Since starting this book, I cannot stop observing the behaviors of people using technology in public places. Sometimes I judge them, but I call it "observing" because it sounds nicer. Most of the time, I am so damn interested in the motivations behind their behaviors. I want to better understand them. I want to know why they are taking a certain picture, openly having a private conversation, or ignoring gorgeous scenery as they scroll Twitter. It fascinates me. I genuinely want to understand it. But noticing people's tech use also improves my habits and my family's habits because it raises our awareness. It gives us a conversation starter. It gives us tangible examples of using technology with purpose. Below I will walk you through several scenes, noting my judgments, perspectives, and insights. What do you think? How do you see it? Does something please or annoy you? Noticing what is happening around you and how it makes you feel is a great way to assess your own beliefs and values. Observing others is a great strategy for strengthening your views and building your family's iRules.

Scene: Adam and I are celebrating our wedding anniversary at a posh outdoor resort restaurant overlooking the ocean on Cape Cod. We snuck away in midmorning with the intention of having lunch and a cocktail and then returning home to our tribe by dinnertime.

Note: *These are celebration strategies used by tired parents on a budget, since lunch is much cheaper than dinner and no one needs to stay up late and miss out on sleep. Because we are in such a luxurious atmosphere, we feel like perhaps we've time traveled, allowing us to fully recharge in a few hours of fantasy. We usually return home to our family all blissed out like we went away on vacation. But we only spent $75.*

Anyway, the table next to us has about seven or eight people enjoying lunch. It seems to be grandparents, a mom, an uncle, and a small group of cousins ages eight to sixteen. There are bottles of wine and plates upon plates of food. It is a gorgeous summer day and the resort is buzzing with swimmers and cabana loungers and satisfied bar guests, all of whom are perfectly dressed and have shiny teeth and good haircuts and ironed clothes. Most seem quite satisfied to be enjoying their vacations at a divine resort during the busiest and most radiant tourist month of the year. At one point after eating, each cousin pulls out an iPhone. This catches my attention. I want to see how the family reacts, how the waitstaff and other resort guests react too. I now watch closely. The youngest one is playing a video game. I can see him twisting and turning, his face showing the same expressions Brendan has when he's playing. Laughing and chatting, the older ones swap phones to look at videos and photos. It is harmless tech use, but the table grows quiet. As the kids plug in, the adults sit idly. I might be overthinking this (I have been known to do this), but it seems to me that a little bit of life has stopped at the table. It bothers me. Here these cousins are on vacation in this magical setting, with plates of good food and beverages in front of them, in spiffy clothes, with living, breathing grandparents right across from them. But their heads are down. They are somewhere else, away from the moment. And maybe because neither I nor my children have ever had family outings or vacations like this one, or maybe because my grandparents, all sacred in my memory, are no longer living, I wish they would just keep their phones in the hotel room and sit around talking about the weather or the box scores or what's for dessert. But they don't. The kids get up before the bill is paid and run off. And I know the phones made it easier for everyone to enjoy this setting. And I know that kids are cuter when they're quiet and occupied and not disturbing the peace. And I know that the mom and uncle and grandparents are trying to relax too. And it looked like no one but me (and Adam, because he has to) really cared about the phones or the early exit. But I saw what could have been!

As a matter of fact, at the very next table was a family of four. There was a little three-year-old girl in a sundress, a sweet baby, and a mom and dad. The little girl sat quietly stacking a tower of blocks her parents had packed. The mom fussed over the baby. The dad was chatting with and encouraging the girl while she was building. Suddenly her straight-line structure leaned and then tumbled down on the table. The waitress laughed genuinely and helped her pick up the pieces. Her parents smiled and set about helping to make the rebuild more stable. It was so refreshing to watch this little girl experiment and play while still being respectful of others. We didn't stay to watch through the end of their meal, but the baby and little girl no doubt grew squirmy and bored. I'm sure the blocks didn't occupy her for hours, but if we give our children strategies to keep busy and engaged during waiting periods and downtimes, they'll become better at it. I saw the scene as this family taking an opportunity for their child to practice being patient and for the parents to meet the child's needs while enjoying their time in a restaurant. I see all the ways it would have been easy to hand over Mom's iPhone, but this deliberate, pre-prepared strategy will strengthen family connections and improve their little girl's etiquette in public settings.

The cousins' use of their iPhones never seemed to bother those at their own table or others around them. But I believe that phones and

 iPhone Contract Success Story
(As told by Gregory)

Greg: Mom! I was having pizza with my basketball team. You called me. I knew I needed to answer your call, but I was also in a restaurant. I panicked for a minute, thinking of the contract—"screen reads Mom," but "restaurant talk is rude." So I decided to step outside and take your call. Then I went back inside when we were done. Pretty good, right?

Janell: Yeah, G! It's that easy! Tangible results—I love when that happens!

devices should be put away in restaurants, especially with children. I think keeping them out builds dependency and detachment. I believe our children can wiggle a bit while we have them sit for a reasonable amount of time. I know that when we take our kids out to dinner, any device use would end up making my children screech and fight. My kids are so much better when the expectation for tech use is clear and direct, with no room for negotiation. Letting them use a device or two would cause so much distraction and discussion among them—and therefore for Adam and me in mediating it—that it would never be worth it to me to introduce one in a restaurant setting (short of providing five devices). No matter how many times I need to play I Spy or remind my kids to sit on their bums, we are a better family when we aren't attacking each other over a video game in public.

iRule Tip: Have you seen rude behavior related to technology use in public? Where were you? Why did it bother you? Discuss those circumstances with your child and ask your child to recall similar situations that they've seen. Help them develop a critical perspective. Create iRules governing public use based on situations you have experienced and witnessed. Kids can apply reasoning and understanding to tangible, real-life experiences.

Work!

iRule: Learn to Earn!

My iRule: If it falls into the toilet, gets smashed on the ground, or vanishes into thin air, you are responsible for the replacement costs or repairs. Mow a lawn, babysit, stash some birthday money. It will happen, you should be prepared.

The day my son got his first iPod for music, when he was about ten years old, he took the dog out for a walk later that afternoon. He had the iPod in his pocket, and when he started running, it smashed on the ground. He had owned it for roughly five hours. It was an absentminded mistake. But this is typical of a child. When we give our children expensive technology, they need to understand the power and sacrifices of that purchase. The iPod lives with a cracked screen to this day. Really!

The feedback I received when my iRules contract went viral was so polarized on the topic of whether or not a thirteen-year-old should have an iPhone. For some families, an iPhone at thirteen is unthinkable for financial, personal, or cultural reasons. In other families, eight-year-olds are given iPhones without hesitation. Many friends and colleagues in upscale metropolitan communities have reported to me that a phone is seen as a status symbol among children. Being without the latest generation would be embarrassing for their child, like not having certain name brand clothes, attending desirable schools, or playing on elite sports teams. Smartphones confer varied levels of perceived sophistication. They represent you.

This got me thinking. Is the pressure to have specific electronic devices really happening only in more affluent communities? I started talking to some of the teens I know, including my own son, in our middle-class neighborhood. And guess what? They answered so certainly that smartphones are the *only* option, that to have a flip phone in eighth or ninth grade would be like wearing "running sneakers to basketball practice—you just don't do it." So much so that my own son said that if he couldn't have a smartphone or iPod Touch, he would rather have nothing at all. I found it fascinating—though not surprising—that our children are being branded with the belief that the smartphone is the only way. When I asked if the brand of smartphone or its generation mattered, they all laughed a resounding "Absolutely." They have a buddy who has an iPhone 1, and they tease him: "When are you upgrading?" "How long have you had that?" This was news to me! I see plenty of people with cracked screens and older models (including myself!) and I never imagined that they are called out on this. The teens I chat with insist that they're kidding around, that they don't really care. It wouldn't stop them from hanging out with these kids or cause them to exclude somebody. But still, they did list the kids—from memory—who either don't have a phone or have an older one. They are so aware!

So what do we do with this expectation? How do we navigate the belief of the typical child that he deserves not just a smartphone, but a certain brand, make, model? I go back to when I considered giving the iPhone to Gregory last fall. I have to ask myself, *Did I feel pressure to get him an iPhone? What was my intention? Did I consider other options?* I know for sure that our decision to purchase an older model was inexpensive, and this was a huge motivation. I know that adding another phone line actually made our data plan less expensive. So cost was not a huge factor. Had I been asked to dish out $200 for the phone, plus a monthly data plan fee of $40 or so, at Christmastime while running a household of seven, Greg would be sitting on his iPod Touch happily ever after—or at least until he could fund a phone himself. Regardless, it was a circumstance of good timing and opportunity for our family. But even then, even when I knew we weren't going to go broke paying for this device, I still wanted Greg to feel that he had to earn his iPhone. And we maintain certain expectations of him in order to keep it. I wanted him to know that his phone is a privilege, not a right. In addition to the iRules contract, I also assessed his household contributions and the costs associated with his activities, which appear below.

Note: *We "wowed" Greg with this exciting Christmas gift, and when the contract went viral, we had to confess that we actually paid almost nothing to give it to him. We had a good laugh about it and Greg was like, "I was thinking to myself, I never thought they'd actually buy this for me!"*

Greg's Household Contributions, January–June 2013

Tech Privileges: iPhone (and all associated apps, social networking, data plan), iTunes downloads, Xbox Live
Financial contribution: $0

Activities: Basketball, baseball, and football registration fees; ski trip; class trip to Six Flags; cleats; batting gloves; four school dance admission fees; and a sprinkling of spending money

Financial contribution: $0

Family System Contribution: Provides frequent child care each week; daily walking of family dog; daily laundry and bed making; weekly room tidying; responsible for the care and replacement costs of all technology and sports equipment; dedicated, responsible student with a near perfect GPA

Financial payment: $0

Assessment: I feel just okay about this. I think Greg is getting older and could probably do more of the heavy lifting considering how generous we are with our money and tech privileges. But he's a good student and we depend on him to help us out with child care.

Are we generous? Are we demanding? It's hard to know what normal is!

Fear alert: I don't want to raise a spoiled brat.

Guilt alert: I don't want to push my kid so hard it's unfair or unreasonable.

Parent from a place of love and balance. Keep searching and working on it until it feels right for you!

List It!

Gather the kiddos! Take inventory of the tech privileges your children have. Take inventory of their interests, their activities, and the associated expenses. Take inventory of their family contributions. It should feel like there is give-and-take. The kids and parents should feel good about what they provide to and what they take from the family system. When our children know the costs and expenses associated with their possessions and activities, I believe we can motivate them to contribute to our households and take ownership. It is perfectly acceptable to require a trade-off or to have expectations for our children when we provide for them.

Part of our daily rounds includes a living list of morning chores. The kids have to make their beds, pick up their dirty laundry, put away their clean laundry, and get themselves completely ready (clothes, teeth, and hair presentable; breakfast eaten; bags packed; etc.). Naturally, my expectations for the result are based on age. Gregory's bed should look better than Cassidy's—yes, *should*. Lily might need help tying her shoes (please don't ever let her read that). I never check my boys' homework because they are old enough to be responsible for it themselves. Ella makes the lunches, but last year she packed marshmallows and carrot sticks for everyone, so I need to be "around" when they're being created.

I noticed the boys had been skipping the bed-making stage. Yes, their middle school bus comes earlier than the girls' bus and they do take out the trash and sort the recycling too, but seriously, I just like them to at least make some effort in caring for the only space in this house that is their own. I volunteered in a shelter in India with girls that were survivors of modern-day slavery. Their beds were in long rows and had gorgeous, colorful bedspreads. They made those beds like professionals, leaving not a wrinkle in sight. They took such amazing, deliberate care of every inch of their beds because they treasured them. Each one's bed was the only thing in the world that actually belonged to her, that wasn't going to be taken away. And despite the trauma and pain they had seen in their young lives, every girl felt like a queen because she had a bed, a space, a home. The girls' pride would vibrate the room when they showed their beds to us. Their beds were sacred. Wow. Okay. Breathe. I do bring this experience to the bed-making table, but still, it's important. I remind them. I set consequences for them and I have to hold to it.

It is work to hold our children to their responsibilities, but it is so valuable to teach them to contribute now, when they are young, and as they grow up. Our households benefit when everyone does their share. Even if there is pushback, it's important to have consistent expectations. How we treat our material possessions, our property—however major or minor—will carry over and impact how we treat the expensive, ever-changing technology.

Busy with a Purpose

The first summer that Greg had an iPhone, I was worried. I knew that naturally, because he was out of school and had less of a set schedule, he would be on it more, on it later in the evening, and connecting with peers that had more freedom too. I was afraid that he would lie around on hot, beautiful summer days scrolling and texting, ignoring the exis-tence of the real world. In the past, we've had limits on video game and screen time for the kids in the summer, but I wondered if Greg's previous cooperativeness on technology use would vanish once he was connected on a personal device. Could our iRules, created during the school year, really hold up during the endless summer days and nights?

The truth is, when I was growing up, I watched a lot of television while I was waiting for "things" to happen. I would babysit regularly, look after my sisters, or read a book, but mostly in the summers from ages eleven to fourteen, I was committed to MTV's *Real World* mara-thons, daytime talk shows, and ridiculous game shows. I played sports and had family commitments, but I just loved zoning out! I can remem-ber slow summer days lumped on the couch with my girlfriends, tak-ing turns talking on the phone to boys we liked or friends who couldn't make it over, the TV blaring in the background. When the heat got too much or we were tired of someone's siblings, we dunked ourselves in someone's pool or walked to the store for a slush. I know for certain that if smartphones had existed, I would have been up to my eyeballs in social networking sites each summer. So it's easy for me to imagine how phones and tablets might grab a kid's attention and keep her eyes on the screen for months. Because of my nature, I feel particularly concerned about how my children spend their time off. So ask yourself the same questions: What did your summers look like when you were a tween or teen? What were the household expectations? What do you want to do differently or the same? Then ask yourself how you can protect your kids' time off. How can you make sure they have freedom and structure during a stretch of time like summer?

Now listen, when I say "structure," I know all about the overscheduled child. I've read about it. I've lived it. I see it every day. I want for my children what you want for yours—for them to become smart, healthy, successful, engaged, accomplished, eager, noteworthy people. I want my kiddos to be all those things too. I know that over the course of their lives, they'll be pretty good at most things, terrible at others, and great at maybe one or two. I've come to terms with that. And all in all it makes me quite happy. So when I say "protect your kids' time off," I don't mean you should sign them up for every Spanish, rowing, or cake-decorating class that comes to town so they're not playing video games all day. I mean keep them engaged—busy with a purpose. Let them explore or volunteer or work or try something new.

And when I say "freedom," I'm not saying you should give your kids a full day to stare at Angry Birds or Instagram as they please. "Freedom" means something different to many families today than it did before. By "freedom" I mean free time with technology, but also free time for open-ended play, riding a bike, swinging, finding a friend, and creating.

For us, it was a perfect match for Gregory to volunteer at a local camp as a counselor in training this past summer. He "worked" three to five days per week from 8:00 a.m. to 4:00 p.m. It was a rustic, outdoor nature camp that serves families in our community. Some things I knew for sure about this experience:

○ He would be outside most of the day.

○ He would be exerting himself physically, and therefore tired.

○ He would be meeting new people—counselors, administrators, parents, children.

○ He would be developing skills such as cooperation, patience, and leadership.

○ He would still have some flexible free time. If some friends were going to the beach or baseball game, he could miss a day without consequence.

○ He would not be on his phone or in front of a screen because devices are not allowed at the camp.

Because our family chose this experience for Greg (all of our other kids attended as campers), it wasn't an issue if he sat using his phone for a while after he came home. I felt that he had worked and contributed to our community and that he deserved to have some time to spend with the technology in whatever way he chose to. When I took an informal poll of some friends on the matters of structure, freedom, and technology in the summer, I was delighted to hear this response from my friend Christine: "My kids have large chunks of structured time during the summer, so I'm pretty hands-off during their downtime. As long as they join us for family activities, read, get their summer school-work done, and get some exercise outside regularly, I figure they have a limited supply of lazy zombie days in their lives."

Another benefit Greg got by working outside all day with children is that this work is known to wear out a young teenager (or anyone!), and most nights Greg headed up to bed by choice long before I had to peel him away from his phone. He was just too tired to care!

When I asked Greg what he had learned and what had been reinforced by spending the summer as a counselor in training, he responded:

○ How to work with kids
○ Responsibility
○ Censorship (appropriate language)
○ Social interaction with co-workers and parents
○ How to treat all people as equals and with respect
○ The golden rule

I must admit, I asked him this on a whim, just to see what his perspective was. And I was thrilled with his response! This is meaningful work for a young person. This is keeping busy with purpose.

To keep your non-working-age teens busy with a purpose, I suggest that you assess their interests: Animals? Sports? Children? Theater? From there, ponder these points to help create structure that will add to and enhance their lives, while still allowing enough freedom for "zombie days" or free play.

Are They Interested in Making Money? Mother's helper, babysitter, regular lemonade stand, yard work, coach, tutor?

○ We know an awesome 11-year-old boy who does couponing and shopping for hire. Each week he tells us the deals, we say what we want, and then he shops for us and we pay him a percentage of the savings! Amazing, right?
○ A mother I know hired a young teenager to go on bike rides and shoot hoops with her active son for two hours twice a week.
○ Ella started a dog-walking business in our neighborhood for dogs under thirty pounds. She charges $2 per walk.
○ Several of Greg's friends spend their summers caddying at the golf course for tips.

Are They Interested in Helping Others?

- I worked with a group of teens that were doing service as part of their leadership program. Each week we went to the local senior center and played board games with the residents.
- Our public library has a puppeteers program for tweens and teens. At the end of the summer program, they put on a show for young children in the community.

Grandparents

I am lucky enough to say that on the summer days when Adam and I were working and the kids did not have camp, their grandparents were a great source of excitement and entertainment for our kids. My in-laws, Bob and Karen, created projects, baked cookies, built things, and carved out nature trails in their backyard and hid treasures throughout it. My mom is a doer. She takes the kids on adventures, seeking fun and madness and food wherever they go. I am too impatient for special projects such as those my in-laws create, and I'm too strapped for time and money to skip out with them on full-day adventures like the ones they enjoy with my mom. Our extended family helps our kids spend their downtime with purpose while building bonds and memories!

Truth: They probably drink soda and watch *SpongeBob* reruns some of the time, but I don't really ask about that because I think grandparents are sacred and get to make their own rules. *As long as they closely resemble my rules, that is.*

Swap

Sharing each other's children is a great way to enhance the connections within our families and communities. During one-week school vacations, my friend Susan and I each choose a day to take the other's girls. I took hers on a hike and a picnic, and Susan took my girls to a local museum. The girls had a playdate or a field trip, and one of us had a break or could go to work. This is a fine example of balancing freedom and structure.

Possessions

When you create an iRules contract for your family, think about how you will handle broken, lost, or stolen devices. I think it's important to identify these boundaries in a Tech Talk before an incident happens. We know dozens of teens that have left their phones at amusement parks, on the hoods of cars, on school buses, at friends' houses, at the gym after practice. Again, it is important to reference the ways you handle the loss or breaking of other material possessions, such as clothes, sports equipment, toys, to work out a solution. You should value devices in the same way. Here are some questions and guidelines to consider and discuss within your family—especially with teens that can contribute financially, handle items with respect and care, and/or actively prevent mistakes.

○ The device drops and the screen cracks. Can the device still function? Does it get replaced or does the child have to live without it?

○ Who paid for the device? Who will replace it? Do you have an insurance plan?

○ Advise your child not to take their phone places where they can't keep track of it or it is likely to become damaged. On Cape Cod, a big one to avoid is the beach: sand, water, sun, teens, crowds—imagine the possibilities!

○ How can your child avoid carelessly losing the device? Have them double-check that they have their phone with them each time they leave school, someone's house, a car, a bus, a restaurant, etc.

○ What if it's stolen? Who is accountable if it's not recovered?

I hear a lot from families that they are worried their children don't understand work or money's value. Many parents feel that today's children are being raised in a culture that teaches them they should get what they want, while working for something and waiting until they have the money for it isn't honored. A reader sent me this via e-mail.

> I definitely have it better now as an adult than [as] a kid, meaning that I can usually buy things when I want to, go on trips, etc. I don't mean that my parents didn't give me what they could, it was just more moderate. But since my kids don't know all this, I don't think they have the perspective I do. We try to tell them that they are lucky, but they see what is going on around them and that most kids are getting what they want in terms of gadgets, sports, and more. My kids get a monthly allowance, but they just need to clean their rooms once a week. I want to change this and help them understand.

I understand this worry too. Both Adam and I were raised modestly. Growing up, I always had enough. My parents had to save and work hard to be able to pay for class trips, athletic fees, and extras. I knew about and respected that pinch, but I never felt that I lacked anything. Often, new clothes, restaurant dining, and our family vacations were paid for by my grandparents. I had to contribute to our family system by doing my schoolwork, participating in athletics, babysitting my younger sisters, and pitching in elsewhere as needed. I was always proud of my family, how they managed and what they taught me and my sisters about hard work, loyalty, and commitment. And I know that my children have more than I did—the value of just the technology they have is higher than that of anything I owned in my entire childhood. Truly! I imagine this is probably the case for most of us. Not to mention the sports fees and playing in the endless private leagues, the extracurricular everything, and that school supplies list! It's an expensive time to raise a family, and now seems as good a time as any to highlight how hard parents work to give things to their children.

I want to raise children that become contributing, high-functioning members of our world. I want them to know how to work, how to earn, and how to make do with what they have. I want them to be able to fight and hang in there when things inevitably get tough, personally or financially. I want them to know sacrifice, to be able to know the gratification to be had in delaying and taking their time. I want them to circle ten items in a catalog at Christmas and understand that they might get just one of the presents they dream of, like we did growing up. I want them to appreciate what is given and to stand proudly with what has been earned.

So every day, I have to make this a priority in my house. I have to make sure my children work and contribute at whatever level is appropriate for the age they are. They must understand how much items cost, know the prices of clothes and food and sports and activities. They must know that we make sacrifices (leopard-print duct tape currently holds up some of our kitchen cabinets) to supply their wants and needs. They need to know they are lucky because their basic needs are met: food, water, shelter, education, health care. They must value what they own by making it last, sharing it with siblings, taking care of it, and not wasting it. I do this not to make them feel bad about or ashamed of having wants or needs, but to teach them how to value things, to make sure that what they have and what they do has meaning to them.

Some Ways to Help Children Understand Value

○   Give them a certain amount of money to put toward sneakers. They can use that to get a pair or apply it toward a more expensive pair they want and pay the difference.

○   Accept and share hand-me-downs. We are very lucky to live in a community that shares clothes, sports equipment, shoes, and all things gently used.

- Learn to wait or live without. Delaying gratifying a "want" helps everyone assess how badly it's needed or wanted. Usually a "want" is temporary. And if not, it's worth saving for!
- Pay the sports registration fees, and have the child pay for the extras—running back gloves, a sweatband, special socks.
- Buy them a new shirt, while they pay for the nail polish or headband.
- Let the kids treat! My friend has four daughters ages four to eleven. They pooled their money to take the entire family out to a restaurant for Father's Day. They were so proud!
- Sell items they have outgrown in order to upgrade. Before we purchased our Xbox, the boys had to organize, price, and sell their Nintendo Wii. They put that money toward the purchase of the Xbox.
- Use cash to pay for groceries, supplies, or gifts. One morning I took some of the kids out to breakfast, to buy each one a new back-to-school outfit, to buy gas, and to go grocery shopping. They watched as the wad of cash I started with at 8:00 a.m. disappeared by 11:00 a.m. Lily said, "Mom, stop wasting your cash on groceries and gas!"
- Teach them not to waste and to only take what they're going to eat or drink. Save some for others.

House Rules and Family Contracts

I bet you make contracts already. I bet your family has sets of agreements that are followed in your house all the time on matters both related and unrelated to technology. After all, there are so many parts of life that are just a series of arrangements and understandings— work, relationships, parenting. When Ella wanted her very own pug puppy, she came to me with a contract she had written on her own.

Well, she said, "a contract worked for Greg to get what he wanted, so it should work for me too." And even though it was almost an entire year before she got the pug puppy of her dreams, I knew that whether she knew it or not, she saw contract making and agreements as strategies to help her intentions be clearly understood and have success with a project or privilege.

 Pug Puppy Contract, Written by Ella Hofmann at Age Eight

- ○ I will walk my dog in all weather before and after school.
- ○ I will brush my dog twice a week.
- ○ I will wash him and his eyes (with help).
- ○ I will feed my dog.
- ○ I will find him healthy food.
- ○ I will give him a quiet place to rest.
- ○ I will help bring him to the vet.
- ○ I will train my dog.
- ○ I will play with my dog.

We both signed the contract and I leave it hanging in the kitchen. Now that Ella does have her own pug puppy (Mr. Blue Berry Hofmann), we often refer to the contract she wrote. If she's sleepy one morning and doesn't feel like walking the dog before school, we tell her she needs to be responsible enough to find someone that will, like one of her siblings. She understands that her willingness to meet these contract conditions was a primary reason we decided to get her Mr. Blue.

Technology and Driving

One of the greatest responsibilities we will ever give our children is the ability to operate a motor vehicle. For decades we have been rightfully worried about proper driver training, the appropriate age to get a driver's license, driving while under the influence of drugs or alcohol, distracted driving, seat belt use, car curfews, ages of passengers, appropriate insurance policies and protection, and so much more. Driving is a rite of passage for so many teens in our culture, but with it comes massive concern and anxiety for parents.

Now, portable technology coupled with its chronic use makes our concerns greater than ever. The statistics are staggering. The risks, unimaginable. When I was growing up, the cultural focus was on drinking and driving. It seemed that most adults in our lives knew that teens, at one point or another, would experiment with alcohol. So instead of imagining that no one would ever go to a party and have a few beers, their message was to never drink and drive or be driven by someone who had been drinking. We heard from Project DARE (Drug Abuse Resistance Education), MADD (Mothers Against Drunk Driving), SADD (Students Against Drunk Driving). I knew certain parents that, when called, would come and pick up their intoxicated child without asking questions to prevent them from driving under the influence. During college I saw the evolution of "designated driver" to "sober driver." During the '90s the prevention of drinking and driving was the cultural focus for young people especially. Through the education of the public and within our own homes, our attitudes were changed by this movement. These strong feelings against drinking and driving remain today. And though we have not erased tragedy or misfortune from drinking and driving, we accept the risks even if we choose to act otherwise.

Recently I interviewed chief of police of Orleans, Massachusetts, and father of four, Scott MacDonald. He said that the prevention of distracted driving is a priority, and that in Massachusetts, it is illegal for drivers under eighteen to use their cell devices while driving. In the state, texting and driving is a primary offense. But he believes all drivers should focus beyond this and avoid anything that distracts them.

So what should parents be telling their new drivers? Properly define "distracted driving." It includes texting, talking on the phone, scrolling social networking sites, selecting music, consulting or searching for maps—even at a red light. If your device requires you to be distracted, pull over. I would tell my children that using a vehicle is a privilege, not a right. That I trust them, but there are consequences to their actions. If they drive a car without following my guidelines, then they cannot drive the vehicle. Even though my children are not driving yet, we still talk about issues involving distracted driving. I have introduced them to the Web site ItCanWait.com, which uses personal stories and celebrity support to consistently send the message that "it can wait." I also try to practice what I preach in the car, but if I do reach for my phone, my kids protest and offer to call, text, or look something up for me. They are already getting and understanding the message about distracted driving.

MacDonald agrees, but he adds, "We have to be reasonable. Our children will have a strong desire to communicate while driving—we all do. It's our culture right now. I would tell your children and my own that they have choices. My expectation is that they have absolutely no phone use in the car unless they pull over to a safe location. I believe they can make that decision if we give them options and teach them to make the right choice."

A distracted driving study analyzing 2011 data was done by the Centers for Disease Control and Prevention. Some of the research concluded that:

○ Sixty-nine percent of drivers in the United States ages eighteen to sixty-four reported that they had talked on their cell phone while driving within the thirty days before they were surveyed.

○ Thirty-one percent of US drivers ages eighteen to sixty-four reported that they had read or sent text messages or e-mail messages while driving at least once within the thirty days before they were surveyed.

○ Younger, inexperienced drivers under the age of twenty may be at increased risk; they have the highest proportion of distraction-related fatal crashes.

○ Nearly half of all US high school students age sixteen or older text or e-mail while driving.

○ Many states are enacting laws—such as banning texting while driving, or using graduated driver licensing systems for teen drivers—to raise awareness about the dangers of distracted driving and to keep it from occurring. However, the effectiveness of cell phone and texting laws on decreasing distracted driving–related crashes requires further study.

So what can we do to keep our children safe behind the wheel when they're driving and when they're riding with others? Just like issues of seat belts, drinking and driving, and speed, it's about conversation and education. Talk about it—the risk, the reality. Set boundaries with clear consequences for violations. Encourage your children to speak up to their driving peers—they can serve as scribe while the driver focuses on the road.

What are working solutions for your family? Is the car a "No Phone Zone"? Set a list of "Do Before You Drive" strategies: Have music cued, maps prepped, and phone silenced before the car goes into drive. We need to normalize the safety (just like seat belt use) around distracted driving with our teens and ourselves. We are the generation of parents that can lead the movement on smart and safe tech use in the car. And it starts with the policies we create in our own homes, with our own children.

iRule Tip: What rules and ideals do you have about valuing material possessions? How do your children contribute to the family system and daily operations of your household? Outline your expectations for your children's contributions to the costs of technology based on your beliefs.

iRule: School

> **My iRule:** It does not go to school with you. Have a conversation with the people you would text. It's a life skill. Half days, field trips, and after-school activities will require special consideration.

Children must learn to use technology in school—it is the future. As parents, we are fed this over and over again: *This is the way. Our children need technology education. We must be certain they evolve and adapt and excel.* And I'm okay with that. I can handle the idea that our kids' classrooms will soon be textbook-free, if they aren't already. That their writing, reading, listening, and sharing will all happen on the same convenient, wildly powerful device. I understand the benefits, the ways our classrooms can connect to the world with ease. I love that access to research is faster than ever and there are endless possibilities and answers for the curious at the touch of a button. But I think we must continue to teach mindful use—even in the classroom.

From the Schoolhouse

It is not always the most horrific stories that rattle us. It is often the small stories that make their way into our lives and our worlds that create the biggest impact. Below are some stories about how technology is creeping into the classroom in ways we didn't anticipate, but we must address. I am not talking about the use of the technological devices that support classroom learning or the benefits of iPads for children with various learning needs. Instead, here we start to see the role we parents play with our chronic communication with our children and the negative consequences of constant connection.

It is open-house night at my son's middle school. Parents pack the auditorium, excited to meet the teachers and peer into the lives of our children, who are rapidly growing more independent. The principal addresses the crowd. She discusses new rules and policies and exciting curriculum additions and introduces new staff. And then she takes a moment and talks about the school's cell phone policy. She says phones are allowed in school, but if they cause a disruption, they will be taken away. She pauses and pleads with parents, telling us that when a phone is confiscated by a teacher, it is almost always because a parent texted a child. The conversation gets serious as she says, "Parents, please do not disrupt your child's school day by texting them during school hours." She goes on to say that the main office has a phone parents can call to leave a message about a change of plans or a need to call home. This system has worked for generations, she says, and she encourages us to continue to use this method of communication to support the staff and limit classroom disruptions.

A junior high school teacher from New Mexico e-mails me in reference to my iRules contract and explains that she is so sad to see how distracted students are during class when they have their cell phones. She explains that for the first time in her twenty-two-year career, students are getting in trouble chronically because of technology disruptions. She also sees children regularly sneaking to the bathroom to watch and share videos or update social networking sites. How do we manage what happens in the school bathroom? She says, "Children that would never under normal circumstances be in trouble in my classroom—good children, from good families—are being reprimanded over and again for being rude or distracted by their cell phones."

A high school English teacher leads a lecture at the front of the classroom. As she diagrams the lesson on the board, her marker falls and she bends down to pick it up. This has happened millions of times in classrooms all over the world. But on this day, a group of students have been using their phones to secretly videotape her. As she bends over, they zoom in. Later that afternoon, the video is posted and shared all over social networking sites, along with vulgar comments and sexual references. The teacher finds out from the administration and is both furious and embarrassed. But she also feels violated and unsafe in her own classroom—the technology has limited her ability to feel at ease and confident in her position.

A fourth-grade girl gets overwhelmed in class one day. She does not understand the math lesson being taught to her by the classroom aide, and she just sits quietly. At lunch, she texts her mother, "I hate this school. I'm having a terrible day. I want to cry. Everyone is so mean." The mother comes to the school and asks the principal and teachers about her daughter's "bad day." When they go together to collect the daughter from the playground during recess, she is happily playing with her friends and says, "Everything is fine now." This child needs to feel empowered to talk to the adults and peers around her when she is upset. Parents need to let their children be at school and work out typical, daily struggles and challenges on their own or with the people around them.

A private junior high school has a no-cell-phone policy that relieves parents of the headaches caused by smartphones in school. But the policy can be impossible to manage. A seventh-grade girl changes her clothes in the school locker room. While her back is turned, another girl takes out her phone and snaps a picture of the girl undressing. She posts it to Instagram. It isn't until hours later that the photographed student looks at her account and sees the shared image. She tells her parents, who help her navigate the rough waters of such harsh adolescent betrayal. While the school did impose a serious punishment on the photo-sharing student, the event left a lasting impact on the privacy of the children involved.

One student in a local district took a photo of a test that he was taking and posted it to Twitter, with a caption that read, "Test is easy." Another high school student is absent from school without permission, but tweets "Chillin' at Dunkin Donuts." The school principal reads it and sends the truant officer to pick up the student. These examples make it clear that our teenagers are not making a connection between what they post online and how it connects them to the outside world or else they wouldn't have done it!

When School Gives Us Technology

I am having lunch in a local shop when a familiar face approaches, a woman I have known for a few years because a couple of our kids went to the same preschool. We both have big families and that brings out a mutual respect and connection, so we always have something to chat about. I know she has a great reputation for being a solid, involved mother and raising great kids.

She looks concerned, vulnerable even, and I am taken aback. I don't think I've ever seen her like this. She takes my hand in hers and thanks me for writing and sharing the iRules contract I made for Gregory. I brush it off with a stock response like "It's been fun!" or "What a wild month!" She pulls me into the corner, serious and stern, and whispers fast and intensely about the struggles she's encountered with her oldest son, a high school freshman, and his nonstop technology use. He too just got an iPhone for Christmas. They have had many conversations about boundaries for its use, but almost immediately he set up a Twitter account behind her back. She felt betrayed. He had no good excuse. She thought they had an open relationship. It doesn't seem like a big deal, she tells me apologetically. But I tell her it is. It's not really about Twitter. It's about control, letting go, risk, trust, and honesty. I can see it in her eyes. She's questioning everything.

She continues. The local high school gave all incoming freshmen iPads. She didn't want the technology in her house. She feels like it was forced on her and her family. Her son doesn't really use it for home-work. He watches Netflix, surfs the Web, and updates his social net-working profiles. She has no interest in learning the technology herself and now her hand has been forced. It doesn't feel fair, she says, because the students and parents had no training. No parental con-trols were set up. There wasn't even a community discussion. Because she takes parenting seriously, she's overwhelmed by the media mad-ness and the invasion of technology into her family and her home. We talk at length about what this means in the larger picture of life, about what is our responsibility and what is natural growth, change, and independence for our children. She asks me with sincerity to continue the conversation. She knows she's not the only mother who feels invaded. She asks me not to let the iRules contract I made for Greg be the end of the conversation and says that we in the parenting com-munity owe it to each other to raise these issues and open the dia-logue. I agree wholeheartedly.

I tell her I'm glad we talked and thank her for her honesty. The more we are real with each other, expressing the truth in our hearts and homes, the more we are empowered to be real to ourselves. We do not need to know all of the answers or suffer in silence. The tech-nology can seem so small that it's easy to brush it off or downplay it, but the issues it presents are vast and only together can we navigate it. We just need the courage to speak up and raise our voices, even if that means starting a conversation in the corner of a sandwich shop. And truthfully, I don't think there's a nicer place to begin.

And so I am inspired to inquire further. At the time, Greg is just a year shy of high school, so I am curious about how other families feel about receiving this iPad or other technology devices from school. How does it transition into the home? Are we talking about it as a family? As a community? Certain I will receive mixed responses—"Technology is the future. Evolve!" and "I'm so furious that no one asked us what our family wanted!"—I dig in.

And just as I'd thought, there are varied degrees of enthusiasm. Here is a small sampling of responses from parents:

○ "So thrilled that our school district supports technology and makes it a priority."

○ "I wish social networking sites were blocked from school-issued devices."

○ "Kids need to learn to self-monitor. I like it happening sooner rather than later."

○ "Too bad that iPads can't be left at school and don't have to come home."

○ "My child only used it for social networking and YouTube."

○ "Teenagers have a hard time resisting the social networking sites during class and teachers have a hard time monitoring it. Vine videos are a popular pastime during classroom hours."

○ "My child's organization really improved—dates, assignments, notes, meetings [were] all on the calendar and easy to manage."

○ "If textbook-free is the goal, then I want my kids to get used to this medium."

○ "A huge distraction."

○ "Parent orientation and family night was a positive way to introduce the home–school technology and the expectations. We were given tools to help us manage it."

○ "I didn't necessarily want this technology in my home and it has needed repairs (thankful for insurance) three times!"

As a mother, I feel this too. My kids recently introduced me to the various tools they use in the classroom (and are offered online at home), and I felt really excited by all of the opportunities, support, and enrichment available. There are limitless tech possibilities and resources to aid and enhance our children's classroom and personal quests for learning. I also believe that the technology helps our children learn by doing, because it is hands-on and user-friendly. My kids love technology.

They love to scroll, swipe, read, press, click whenever possible. I believe the technology engages them. I love that. It makes me bounce in my seat—it enables fast, fun, driven, excited learning. Hooray! But I don't want the technology to replace their human experiences and interactions. So I start asking myself, *What is important to me that my children get in the classroom? What skills do I want to preserve in their learning?* I create a list of skills that, even with the highest and mightiest technology available, I believe to be invaluable.

I speak to several educators working directly with special needs students. And I am surprised by what I consistently hear. I am told that with technology, the possibilities for enhancing the education and experiences of children with special needs are endless. There are apps assisting with speech, language, voice recognition, letter recognition, daily schedules, emotions, feelings, names of objects, photos of people in their lives, activities, comprehension, and more. But what sticks with me the most during these conversations is feedback like this comment from one special education teacher of children up to six years old. She says, "Nothing can replace play at this age for developing imagination, social skills, pre-reading skills, and life skills. However, when used appropriately, technology can be very positive. It is now readily available, easier to use, and more socially acceptable. But the technology is replacing play, is often used as a babysitter, and does not allow for the development of social skills." Another teacher gives similar feedback. "Parents and educators need to be reminded to use a variety of methods in teaching [all] children. Books, hands-on activities (like cooking and games), environment, and experiences need to be used along with any technological device." I think it is fascinating that so many parents, professionals, and educators that work with children consistently agree that tech use needs to be balanced and mindful.

I continued connecting with educators of all disciplines working with children of all ages and abilities. Again, the responses were consistently promoting a balance. Many teachers believe that if they are properly trained and given curricula that work with the technology, then devices in the classroom make them more effective and efficient professionals. They have more energy to help and assist students, they don't lecture as much, and students can move forward or continue working at varied paces. But many educators feel that the technology is one step ahead of the curricula and are not entirely confident about

 ## Slow Tech Parenting Tools

○ Have pencils, paper, stamps, envelopes, tape, glue, rulers, and scissors easily accessible and available. Cope with the temporary mess of creation.

○ Make homemade birthday cards and valentines. Even messy, horrible ones with lots of scribbles. They don't have to be Pinterest quality. Send a letter!

○ Have library cards for the whole family, and take regular trips to a public library to explore the (free!) joy to be found there.

○ Make buying and receiving a book a special occasion or reward.

○ Have lively, engaging family discussions for all ages. Ask questions, give opinions, model and teach respect for both sides in a disagreement, give examples.

○ Let the kids figure it out! Make a list of chores and say, "Divide them up and get everything done by noon." See who leads, who delegates, who works well with a partner or independently. Let them fight it out and conquer the work on their own.

○ Have blocks and puzzles freely available.

implementing classroom technology to its full potential because they are uncertain of how to use it or because it is a new, unfamiliar way of teaching. Additionally, like some of the parents, teachers believe social networking sites and texts being sent during school time are distractions that are hard to manage.

We also see a shift that makes teachers responsible for managing classroom social networking sites. The expectation in a tech-savvy school district is that each teacher will post pictures and other content to the class site every day. This helps keep parents engaged and motivates staff to highlight their daily lessons and practices. I have talked with many teachers that feel obligated to take out their phones and snap photos or tweet during class time. The pictures span schoolwide assemblies, science fair projects, group work, and independent reading. Some teachers feel like the sharing and home–school communication encourage them to make every moment exciting and engaging and that the sharing helps strengthen the bonds among students, teachers, and parents. But with all aspects of the school day being documented and shared, a moment now can't be missed, and teachers are often pulled away from observing or walking with the class to snap a picture and post it in real time.

Everything I Want My Kids to Learn

○ They think for themselves. Even if it's only for a few minutes, I want them to rattle around a question or thought in their minds before seeking the answer online.
○ They can ask for help—from another person.
○ They can write with a pen or pencil or crayon or marker on paper.
○ They know and appreciate the value of holding a book, whether it's a used book all dusty and well loved, a crispy new book just creaked open, a library book, a book fair book, any kind of book!

○ They can have a conversation, argument, or discussion with peers in person.

○ They can problem solve and work with people on a team.

○ They can sketch or build something representing an idea or concept. (Well, this is Adam's input here. Building blocks and protractors aren't my strengths, but I appreciate their value.)

○ They listen. They know how to sit long enough to have a story told to them or a concept explained.

And so what happens if these traditional forms of student experience fall by the wayside? And even if they don't, what if some families don't nurture or appreciate them with the same passion that I have for them? How can I make sure my family embraces the evolution of classroom learning and preserves the parts of education that I found beautiful and engaging? I would need to be deliberate about keeping the balance.

Revise!

This iRule is the only one that Gregory amended when he initially reviewed the contract. Originally it said, "It does not go to school with you." He asked if he could bring his phone to school if he had a sports event after school or a field trip where he might want to listen to music on the bus or take pictures. Because I thought this was a good point that I had not considered, I agreed to the change. It is appropriate to discuss iRules with our children. We want their participation and input. A partnership like that will help them take ownership of the iRules. Parents all over the globe have been connecting with me about adaptations and additions they have made for their children and suggested I make them too! Here are some of the suggestions:

○ Do not text and drive.

○ Do not drive while distracted.

O   Do not stay in a car with a texting or otherwise distracted driver.

O   Do not give your password to anyone.

O   Limit the amount of time the phone is against your head.
Use an earpiece.

This is a teachable moment. This contract isn't as authoritarian as it might seem. In my *Good Morning America* segment with *GMA* consultant Josh Shipp of Lifetime's *Teen Trouble,* Shipp said that negotiations and dialogue are vital parts of good relationships and foster respectful discussions. Additionally, he agreed that, just as we wouldn't give our teens keys to the car without driving lessons, we shouldn't give our children technology without rules. It's important that parents and children come together regularly to reassess their iRules contract, especially those related to children's contributions to the home and schoolwork. So much in a family's life can change with sports and extracurricular activity seasons, teachers' requirements, workloads, parental commitments, and family needs that our contracts need to have fluidity so they can adapt with our expectations.

iRule Tip: How is my child as a student? How will having a portable electronic device in school help or enhance the experience? Is my child easily distracted by the device? What is the school's policy on its use? These are all important questions to ask when deciding whether to allow at-home technology to go to school.

5

Sex and Technology

iRule: Preach Safe Text!

> **My iRule:** No porn. Search the Web for information you would openly share with me. If you have a question about anything, ask a person—preferably me or your father.

Sexuality and curiosity about it are normal parts of adolescent development. We know this much for sure. At first I wanted to open this chapter with all sorts of porn stats and details, but most of the research is dated and it's hard to track down accurate sources. See, if I told you about the price tag on the global porn industry (billions of dollars) and the number of page views, searches, shares, and the duration of time spent on porn sites, you would fully understand and agree that people spend money buying and watching porn. But because you probably knew that already, I won't carry on. I really hope this is not the first time you're learning: *Porn is popular and the Internet has made it easy to get.* I hope this is understood. If not, I'm glad I could enlighten you. Porn and the Internet are like peas and carrots.

But I also want you to know that those billions spent don't account for all of the porn that's available. There's been a large increase in free porn, and it has yet to be measured accurately or traced by demographic. I want you to know that most studies and articles say that eleven used to be the average age when most kids see porn for the first time, but now research is beginning to show that because of increased use of and portable technology, that age has dropped closer to eight. School-age children are accidentally stumbling across porn doing homework, searching for games or videos, and sharing messages and pictures with peers. Even teens that don't go looking for porn are seeing it more than we ever did, because, well, it just happens to be where they are—online. And the teens that do want it—well, for them, it is everywhere and accessible.

And then I was going to get all moral on you. I wanted you to know that porn isn't natural, it's staged. Porn often depicts women as objects or victims. Women are the decoration, and stories are often told through the male gaze. Women are not meant to receive pleasure, but to act like it's the most amazing moment of their lives, even if it's weird or painful. I took all the gender studies classes I could, read theories and books, watched documentaries, and listened to interviews about the sex industry. Many porn actresses admit to childhood trauma having been their path to the industry. I believe women can choose to earn money however they want to, but the choice must be made as an independent, free-thinking human being, not one who is forced or coerced into it by addiction, threats, or a lack of alternatives. I want you to know that, yes, the women in porn movies are someone's sisters, daughters, mothers, living in the world and dealing with life like the rest of us. And I know that absolutely no one thinks about these details when they are watching or looking at porn, partly because you know all of this already and partly because porn is so good at doing what it does best and sexual arousal can supersede all rational or critical thought. But sometimes when I see a stripper or porn actress, all I can do is wonder—what's her story? Because I know she has a powerful one. And when we start seeing people for who they really are, well, what we want to tell our children becomes pretty damn clear: Sex is more than porn.

Instead of statistics or morality, I will tell you what I really think is important. We need to reflect on where our children are getting their information. In a time of porn apps and the hype of "porn culture," technology should never replace the information we provide for our children. If we do not take the time to teach our children about sexual health and behavior in a way that is based on our own family values and beliefs, they will learn false truths about what is healthy and real through their (often unlimited) access to the Internet. Pornography must be part of the technology discussion. We must have iRules that are in line with what our family beliefs and values are when it comes to sexuality and technology. Porn is here, all around us. Start evaluating your family's perspective on it, start to fold the topic into the discussion about permissible tech use.

Fact: You will have to parent porn, like it or not.

Both Gregory and Brendan have seen porn videos or pornographic images. I know this for sure because I accidentally happened upon the scene a few different times. They've also talked to me about some of the sexual images, discussions, and posts they've seen online. Certainly, I do not know everything. Nor do I want to! Eeek! I just want them to know this very basic concept: Curiosity, sexuality, and arousal are natural and most of what they see online is not. Our discussions and experiences can branch out and deepen from this point.

Some of the iRules contract criticism I received suggested that my "no porn" iRule point might have somehow embarrassed or shamed Greg. I feel strongly that I did not provide him with an iPhone so he could view porn. That was not and never will be my intention. I was being clear and direct on that matter. He knows that. Do I think that he will? Perhaps. Do I understand the temptation? Absolutely. But my guideline directs that this device, gifted to him, is not for such purposes. The phone is to be kept "clean," and that is our agreement.

Let's Talk about Porn

So, recently I was hiking for the day with a group of women. Some of them I have known for years, some are acquaintances, and some I had just met. They asked me about the book, and the conversation that followed went like this.

> **Friends:** Janell, what part of the book are you working on?
>
> **Me:** Porn and teens.
>
> **Friends:** *Laughter, followed by silence.*
>
> **Me:** Seriously?! Everyone does this to me! No one will tell me a damn thing about porn! If I asked you about video games or *Minecraft* addiction in your ten-year-olds, you wouldn't shut up. But I say "porn" and everyone takes a vow of silence.
>
> **Friends:** Well, we don't know what to say. We have young kids. We haven't really been there or done that. It's overwhelming to think of the kids seeing that stuff even by accident—never mind when they go looking for it. We only have husband porn stories *[TMI re husband details ensue]*. We can tell you one thing: There is a ton of free porn on the Web!

We carry on. I decide to take a different approach. I ask them about the first time they saw porn growing up. Not one person I have ever asked this question has failed to answer—male or female. Everyone has a strong memory of this. And truthfully, the collective memories are similar: a magazine stolen from someone at home or a relative, or found lying on the road, at a friend's house, crumpled up behind a

Dumpster or at the playground, or a rogue VHS played at a junior high boy–girl party, at a sleepover, with some older kids. All of it done in secret, most of it photographs in a magazine or a scratchy videotape with the volume on silent in a basement. The reactions remembered are almost always similar too—curiosity, arousal, embarrassment, discomfort, shame. Put those feelings in a blender, and our first display of sexuality becomes all mixed up.

The conversation continues. We talk about our first experiences, most impromptu and brief, compared to our generation of children. The accessibility to pornography is so easy. Children walk around carrying devices on which porn is just a click away at any given moment. It can be hidden, secretive, and isolated like anything done on a personal device, away from the eyes of adults. We talk about today's high-definition images, camera angles, the variety of options—one of the women laughs as she remembers trying so hard to see the sex scenes and naked people in movies through the squiggly lines of subscription cable channels growing up. This was not that long ago! No one in this group is even forty! Yet so much has changed in such a short time—human curiosity has stayed the same, but the access and availability are quite different. We talk about advertising, the sexualization of culture, what our expectations are for our own families.

This is a good conversation. But too often it is one that is hidden. Parents are embarrassed to admit or share that their children have seen porn or are interested in sex. It can feel like a violation of family privacy (always keep respect for your child a priority). Again we ask, what is normal? What does it say about my level of supervision or my morals? How do we talk about this? But connecting with other parents, sharing our fears and concerns, can help moderate what is boiling over in our minds. Most of our children are typical, finding their way with successes and missteps. Parents need support to navigate changes and behaviors in things related and unrelated to technology. Don't be afraid to connect with others about sexuality and parenting. Let's stop hiding this conversation from each other and from our children. It's a great way to be sure the technology is being used for healthy habits and behaviors.

We all have differing degrees of "porn tolerance." Some families think that porn is no big deal and a part of life. Some families say "absolutely not" to their children accessing it, viewing it as sinful. Most people I talk to know that their children will experiment with porn. But how we—their parents—talk about porn, sexuality, relationships, and health will impact them greatly. What we choose to say, how we choose to behave, and the conversations we create will guide them through all of their usage choices with the technology, including the porn.

Often we find ourselves parenting an emotionally hot topic like porn. The situations often have a lot to do with circumstances aside from porn—sneaking, lying, ignoring rules about content that has

 # My Porn Tolerance

I don't want my kids accessing porn. Bottom line. I don't think it's healthy, it's not where I want them to get their ideas or beliefs about sexuality. I want them to build connections (yes, even sexual ones) with themselves or real people. But despite my feelings, they probably will view porn anyway. I believe there will be times in their lives when they are curious enough to go looking for it, are put in a situation with it, and even (the horror!) enjoy it. But my hope is that they don't need to rely on it, that their use of it isn't chronic, that they understand they are watching sex acts staged for one sole purpose and it's not about love. I hope that their world is so full and busy and beautiful that they don't need porn as a central outlet.

been agreed upon as forbidden. Direct conversations are best. Don't make it messier than it needs to be! We have to be brave enough to stop and ask ourselves what the real issue is and how we want to respond. We don't want our kids to associate sexual feelings with shame, but we do want them to have parental guidance and consequences to deal with if they have not followed the rules. This leaves me with only one choice, and that's to give you a real scene from my very own life.

Parenting Porn: Take One

Gregory was about eleven or twelve in the sixth grade.* One weekend afternoon he asked to use my laptop upstairs in my office to "look for something." I said sure without thinking too much about it. Meanwhile, I was using the iPad with my girls to look up Pinterest projects (not for me to complete, just for me to envy). We stumbled across some unbelievable birthday cakes, in particular a cake decorated to show the balloons, house, and characters in the Disney movie *Up*. It was amazing! In seconds I ran up the stairs, iPad in hand, to show Greg this masterpiece. As I entered the room, he got this panicked look on his face and shut the screen quickly. I froze. He froze. I said something ridiculous like "Are you looking at naked people?" He said something ridiculous like "Yes." *Nooooooo! My baby! My angel! My precious!* But I only thought those things, I did not say them. Instead, I said this: "It's okay. I'm going to leave the room. Why don't you close the Web site and any other windows you were looking at and come downstairs?" I was shocked, but he was mortified. Downstairs a few minutes later, we sat down. I needed to process. He said some friends had mentioned a Web site and he was curious. It was only still images, not videos. He thought the woman would be "just" naked, but it turned out that the photos were quite graphic, and included "stuff I didn't want to see." I found the Web site later that night by looking at the browser's history, and it left me in agreement with him—intense! It was more like an anatomy lesson than a sex scene. But anyway, we talked about pornography (again), and I did point out that he had been on *my* computer. Yes, the tool I use to write and earn money, and porn can be virus central. I told him I love him no matter what. And just to be sure, I asked Adam to take him for a solo car ride the next day to talk about the situation, and about sex. I am very comfortable talking to and teaching my children about sex, but I think it is vital that Adam plays a major role in building our children's sexual health too.

---

*Story shared with Gregory's permission

How to Talk to Your Teen or Tween about Pornography

○ Explain that pornography is a multibillion-dollar industry that sells sex. Tell them it is normal to be curious about, interested in, and aroused by pornographic images and videos. That is the entire point! But it is about more than just sex. Then open the conversation.

○ Ask your child if they have ever seen pornography. Tell them about the first time you saw a porn magazine or movie. The more embarrassing for you, the better! The shared laughter will disarm your child and perhaps shift the conversation from a lecture to an "I've been there."

○ Talk about the changes in pornography. Talk about accessibility. Share your porn experiences with your child. Discuss the social changes that have taken place in the pornography industry since it has been available on the Internet. Let them know that we didn't walk around with access to porn on our smartphones like they do!

○ Tell them the adults shown in pornography are actors and actresses, that they are used as props to promote sexual arousal. If your child is still hanging in with the conversation, tell them that most of the sex acts seen in pornography are not being enjoyed by the people in it. The images are being cropped and edited to make it look like the actors enjoy the sex act.

o Tell them about all the things men and women do like about sex—the deep connection, trust, arousal, passion, excitement, orgasm—and that it's all okay and natural. And that while porn is a part of our culture, it does not depict a loving, healthy sexual relationship. I also always throw in a bit about the power of imagination and creativity when developing into a sexual being and avoiding being dependent on the porn world or someone else's idea of what is sexy or exciting.

This is precisely the point when my children say "Mom! Okay! We get it. We get it. Stop." Then they like to mumble under their breath that I get "carried away" and "creep [them] out with details." But that usually means they heard me and understood. We always have a few laughs at my expense.

Truth!

I work with and adore a lot of teenagers and young adults. I have built trusting relationships with them and engaged in a lot of varied conversations, and I am always delighted in their willingness to share stories with me about their lives. However, there has never been a time when I thought asking them about their porn habits, interests, and behaviors was appropriate, like it does when I ask about their passion for texting or Vine video making. In certain circumstances—my work with girls and young women, for example—I can tell them what porn is, how it's created, and what its relationship to mass media is. But it is up to you— the parents and family—to speak to your children and teens about porn and your family values in relation to it. No one else would (or should) have this conversation for you. It is deeply personal and potentially awkward, but these are the times where we earn our stripes as parents: when we push our fears, hang-ups, and discomfort aside to reach out to our children. They will squirm and tell you to stop. Get your point across; hang in there! They need to hear about the world from you. Even if they cover their ears, show them your courage.

Not Just Porn

We really do want to protect young children from pornography. It is hard for them to understand or explain porn, and we certainly don't want anything they see online to be their introduction to sexuality. We want to work very hard to preserve their innocence, and pornography can be scary and confusing for a young child. In the event that they do come across sexual images and ask you about them, be clear and direct. For example, ask them, "What did you see? Do you have any questions about what you saw? Sometimes people post pictures and videos of themselves doing all kinds of things with their bodies—including sexual things. I'm sorry you had to see that. I will make sure that doesn't happen again. You didn't do anything wrong, but I understand if you feel confused [or angry, scared, curious, funny]."

In addition to porn, there are many other scary things our young children can accidentally come across in a simple online search. Sometimes the images are real and sometimes they are altered or edited. A child cannot always understand the difference, and it is hard to "unsee" what has been seen. Millions of people use the Internet as a form of self-expression. The most important thing we can do is to prevent our children from accidentally coming across something inappropriate. This can be done by using parental settings* and either supervising or being nearby your children when they're online.

---

*Most devices come with easy-to-use instructions on parental settings, and there are a wide variety of apps available to help too. A quick Internet search will provide you with a sea of suggestions. Parental controls should always be used in addition to your own real-life boundaries.

Times of Tragedy

During times of tragedy that involve peers or nearby communities, or more distant catastrophes that are big news stories, I've noticed that the tweens and teens I know tend to up their social networking usage. I watched this play out during the Boston Marathon bombings. It was hard not to be glued to the news. At one point, doctored pictures and graphic images were being shared. It was very intense for young people (all people!) to process the bombings because they were fully immersed in it, never putting their phones down. Situations like these are great times to limit kids' technology use or be more aware of how it is being used. Talk to your children about what they are seeing and experiencing. Ask about their thoughts and feelings. Remind them that not everything they see or read is accurate and introduce them to reputable news sources and Web sites for information.

With events on a local scale, information tends to travel quickly through social networking sites. Kids might hear about a car accident, a friend's sports injury, or a teacher's personal life through social networking. Teach your children how to use tact. Teach them to be certain they have accurate information. I've seen kids immediately rally around a person, situation, or family by using a hashtag to start a support movement, like #prayforJohn. And that's okay, because it feels good to be part of a community. Just be certain your children aren't sharing others' personal tragedies or situations online and that their love and support are consistent with what the family wants and what is appropriate for the incident.

When Cassidy was in preschool, she was searching for *Sesame Street* videos on YouTube. She was proud to be able to do this on her own. I didn't realize that some of the videos available aren't authentic and show some of the characters swearing or using fresh language and their faces are distorted. Luckily, I was nearby and could tell something wasn't right because of their voices. Even though the inappropriate part passed by quickly and Cassidy hardly processed it, I still couldn't help but think about what she might have seen had it kept playing or if she had happened upon a worse video. I'm an adult, and I've seen some pretty disturbing images online! Imagine how confused a child can feel.

As our children get older (say, seven and up) and start to use search engines and devices when we are not physically present, we want to make sure they are safe. This is an important consideration to focus on in your own iRules. In our house, Ella and Lily cannot stream a television show or movie without permission. They cannot search without letting me know the subject. They must ask to download an app (even a free one!) or song, and they do not know the password for purchases. These are part of our iRules to help keep them safe and build a healthy relationship with technology. Keeping an ongoing dialogue going is key. "What games did you play online today?" "What songs did you listen to?" Every once in a while it is important to ask questions like "Have you ever seen anything online that you didn't like or that confused you?" This promotes conversation and dialogue about sometimes uncomfortable subject matter. It's practice for the years ahead, and it allows a child to know that it is safe to come to parents and people they trust if they are ever confused by or unsure about something they see online.

When Brendan was about nine, he came home from a friend's house cranky—stomping, arguing, resisting—just not himself. When I saw this behavior, I asked, "What did you do at your friend's house today?" He moaned about his friend having been just "staring at his computer." A lightbulb went off. I follow up with "What was he watching or playing?" A part of me already knew the answer by the way Brendan was acting. He said he didn't want to talk about it and added a bunch of rambling sentences including the words "hate" and "dumb" and "stupid" all rolled together. I let it fall quiet between us for a few minutes, giving him a chance to answer. I asked, "Was he looking at inappropriate stuff? Like sex pictures?" And then the tears flowed out. I comforted him. I told him he didn't do anything wrong. That those pictures on the computer are confusing and I could understand why he was upset at his friend for looking at them when he was there to play. He settled down and I could see the relief in his eyes. It made me sad. I knew that a pinch of his innocence had been lost and it was completely out of my control.

You can't prevent everything. It's almost impossible to even try to prepare for everything. But when open discussion is weaved into the family's life when the children are young, these conversations don't feel forced or contrived as they turn into teens. It continues to flow when we encourage our children all along. And yes, sometimes we need to push and give a little to help the conversation along, especially when it's sticky or the kids feel like they may get in trouble. We have to be delicate sometimes and forceful others. But, above all, we* need to be there.

---

*By we, I don't exclusively mean parents. I mean grandparents and caregivers and teachers. I mean caring, present adults. In no way should parenting all of this madness fall to one gender or one role.

When I created the original iRules contract for Greg, it wasn't the first time we had discussed the contract's points. We had been talking all along. The main reason he took the media frenzy that followed in stride was that he understood the points clearly, why they were part of the conversation, and why they were important to our family. He had been raised on the philosophies at the basis of the contract, even though in this specific instance the subject matter was technology. Throughout Greg's life we have been talking about television programming, commercials, computer games, video games—what they mean, how they relate to how we live. Even a preschooler can understand and make a connection to a commercial that shows "boy toys" and "girl toys." We just need to support that connection with starters like "Why do they only show boys playing with trucks?" or "Don't you think boys like making crafts too?" If we encourage our children to look critically at media (anything, really!) in an age-appropriate way, it will have a lasting impact on how they process everything in their world.

iRule Tip: Think about how you got your information about sex when you were growing up. How well informed were you? What were the beliefs and behaviors around sexuality that you were taught? How did it impact you? Now think about your child. What do you want them to know that you never learned (or learned too late) about their powerful bodies as sexual beings and navigating the influence of the world on them? It doesn't have to be perfect, but it should be authentic and deliberate. If you don't teach your children about sex within the beliefs and truths of your family, they will learn it somewhere else. It's easy to begin with everything you wish you knew!

iRule: Practice Safe Text

> **My iRule:** Do not send or receive pictures of your private parts or anyone else's private parts. Don't laugh. Someday you will be tempted to do this despite your high intelligence. It is risky and could ruin your teenage, college, and/or adult life. It is always a bad idea. Cyberspace is vast and more powerful than you. And it is hard to make anything of this magnitude disappear—including a bad reputation.

"Selfies"

Tweens and teens (and adults!) are known for taking "selfies"—self-portraits—and then sharing them online. Most of the selfies I see are harmless—mirror reflections of the person in a favorite outfit, or close-ups after getting a new haircut, while enjoying a meal at a restaurant, at the beach. Selfies can be serious, silly, artsy, or just regular pictures. It is fun for people to put their "I am here" stamp on experiences and adventures. And I get that. My biggest selfie complaint is that it's overused: "Really, another one?" A self-portrait might be shared to sometimes dozens—often hundreds—of friends' social media pages multiple times a day or week. And they can be peculiar. Personally, I am uncomfortable with the selfie. Since you take the photo of yourself, it's usually no more than arm's length away or a mirror reflection of you standing. Every selfie I've ever taken has been totally unflattering. Self-portraits hardly convey the experience or message, and I feel awkward sending it out into the world in a "look at my face!" kind of way. But I'm an adult. I tend to like to find meaning or purpose in things, and I'm careful not to over-post on my social networking sites (unless the photos are of my kids because they're especially cute). It's not my style, but I'm not a quitter, so I might keep practicing. And sometimes it looks fun! After all, it is the way—a very common way—for people to communicate and share the events in their lives through texts and on social networking sites.

However, there are other ways in which the selfie is used (and abused). Selfies of typical teens in sexual poses or postures are becoming more and more popular and are being posted and shared all over the Internet: the girl just out of the shower wrapped in a towel, the slumber-party braless pajama pics, the cleavage while lying on a beach towel are becoming classics. Then there's the pouty face, the arched back, the bending-over pic taken from behind. Getting these angles takes practice, people! And somehow these sexual selfies of images seen in our homes' mirrors leave our houses, work their way behind the privacy of closed doors, and wind up on the phones and computers of every peer our child interacts with. And it's not just girls doing it.

It is the summer of 2012 when I first notice that Instagram is becoming popular with Gregory's peers. I've been using it for only a few months. The pictures of the people I follow are consistently unimpressive—a screenshot of a Will Ferrell tweet my son loved, my neighbor's adorable baby in a watermelon bathing suit, my high school classmate's puppy napping in the sun, a family friend's foaming latte. Looking at it is a fun, distracting way to pass a few minutes here and there. Everyone has a chance to be artsy with the filter selections and color enhancers. I like it enough to look at it every few days. I like to see what my son and his buddies are up to since we all follow each other. It feels like a safe place to be in tune with them without invading their space. But I'm not really locked into it.

During this time, I see that posts of young teen and tween girls' selfie-style bikini pictures are becoming the norm on social networking sites. Are they really just showing off their new or favorite suits? Or is the motivation different? Certainly, this is a common age to start experimenting with behavior that may have a little "kick" or thrill to it. There are often dozens of likes and comments: girls exclaiming to one another "beautiful," "amazing," "hot," and some boys having the courage to put emoticons of smiley faces or the thumbs-up. Am I out of touch and overreacting? I wonder if their parents know. I wonder how I will feel when Ella is this age. If Greg was flexing or posturing in his bathing suit, would I have the same reaction? I wouldn't love it being out in cyberspace, but I probably wouldn't feel as concerned. Is this a double standard for our daughters? What's the responsibility of our sons here in terms of liking, commenting, saving, and sharing these pics? How can we be sure everyone has some accountability? I can't

 ## Mom and Dad, Close Your Eyes

During high school, I engaged in risky behaviors like sex and drinking. I had a fresh mouth. I loved older boys and loved having a good time. Every now and then, for no good reason, I'd take my shirt off at a house party to kick up the fun. I understand the thrill of risk. I get the thrill of being looked at and getting attention, even if it's just suspending reality and not done often. But it was different. It wasn't public. No one took pictures, never mind shared or posted them. It couldn't follow me. The way I behaved among friends or at a party here and there during high school didn't define me, it didn't appear forever on my profile. It happened, and then I went back to being the more complete version of myself—an honors student, an athlete, a good friend and daughter—a typical, well-rounded teenager.

seem to find a way to get comfortable with this. How will I know where the picture ends up? How will I know the true motivation behind the post? Can we trust our young teens' judgment on behaving in a way that protects and respects them and shows they have a complete understanding of the consequences and intentions?

I know I am not a prude. They're not naked. It's not pornographic and not always sexual in nature. I took a lot of risks as a teenager, and in this moment I'm forced to reflect on them, to soothe myself with my own experiences. What is normal? What is typical limit testing and coming-of-age experimenting, and what crosses a line? I suppose we all have our own parental sense of what feels "right" to us and for our children. The key is knowing and enforcing that.

Our children on social networking are often quite young and the pictures are on display in a way that feels both public and permanent. I show some other adults I trust to gauge their reactions to bathing suit pic sharing. Everyone is concerned about the trend. I'm bordering on horrified because I know it will become the norm. It's a slippery slope sometimes with online behaviors—and with all of our behaviors and choices: They lead somewhere. My dad used to say to me, "If I let you [insert one of the many things I begged to do] at fourteen, what will you want to do at sixteen or eighteen? We need to go slowly and carefully or else you will grow up too fast." Which of course I did anyway, because I was determined to grow up fast, so I really do understand the motivation! I often think about my dad's insight in my own parenting journey, and if posting certain pictures at age twelve or fourteen is common and mainstream, what, then, is common or mainstream at sixteen and eighteen? Does the risk become greater? Are choices more or less responsible? I care, even though at this moment in my parenting, my awareness is heightened because I can really only control what happens in my own home and talk about my expectations.

For weeks, I feel all tangled up about the possibility that these sometimes sex-oriented self-portraits are generally accepted. I wonder what happens to a girl's self-esteem if she doesn't get the number of likes or the praise she was hoping for. I wonder if she gets a rush out of it, a charge, or if it feels like no big deal at all. This reality of the direction our children are headed in feels huge to me. I am scared to ask what's next; the changes in technology and behaviors related to it are inevitable. But sometimes my imagination can get carried away, making things feel heavy and serious to me. I want to preserve and extend the purity of childhood. I don't want twelve-year-olds worrying about sharing cute bikini pics (even though I probably would have!). It means more to me to stay present in this space, trying to understand it all, while thinking critically about what feels right for my family. I hold all children close to my heart and hope that one zillion likes means nothing compared to how they feel about themselves inside.

As I reflect on this memory of my first introduction to risky tween photos roughly two years ago, I think about all that I have seen and heard since. I wonder if I would even flinch at some of those pics if I saw them today. (The answer is still a resounding yes.) I have seen the boundaries pushed and the risks increase over these two years. I have heard stories and watched teens make so many choices online every day that walk right up to (and often cross) the line. And this is proof to me that we become accustomed to new behaviors and start to accept them as typical. Something that once outraged or confused us, we now accept. Hold true to your initial instincts—those are your values speaking. Carry them with you always on this journey of parenting.

Once, Ella stole Brendan's iPod and took a bunch of super close-up selfies. Brendan later found them saved on the iPod and showed them to me (to tattle on her and to make fun of her). She had taken all of the classic pics—peace sign, duck face, surprised face, serious face. HOW DID SHE KNOW HOW TO DO THIS? SHE'S NINE!! She has no social networking accounts and no access to devices to see them on. Why does my child know how to pose for selfies? I doubt Greg has ever even let her glance at his news feeds, never mind study how his female friends

Say This about Selfies!

- O I want to see your eyes.
- O I want to see your face.
- O I want to see your smile.
- O I want to see the parts of you that are whole.
- O I do not want to see inappropriate portions or sections of you.
- O Every picture you post of yourself must include your face—that is the real you! Unless it's a fancy pedicure or a bruise you earned in a close game, which of course are exceptions!

pose. Aunts? Babysitters? Television? Big sisters of friends? She's paying attention and absorbing. And even though we thought it was funny, it opened my eyes to the messages that she is receiving about our culture and what is accepted and expected. Kids know the scoop. Make sure you do too!

Sexting

I am wildly excited, thrilled really, that my adolescent and young adult years did not occur after the invention and spread of the smartphone and camera phone. I would love to say that I never would have said or done anything that would have put me at risk for regret or shame, but that would be a lie. I think of the conversations, the parties, my nothing-can-stop-me developing brain, and I know for certain I would have made choices that were not in my best interest for the long road (or the short one). If you disagree or think your teenage or young adult self would have been above sending a sext message, party pic, or trusting nudie, I think you are full of it. Really.

I don't see it as unfathomable that teenagers and young adults send and receive sext messages and sexual pictures. I see it as a reality in our culture and I want to empower as many families as I can to discuss it and the consequences it can have. I feel so strongly, so passionately, that we must have these conversations with our children. It is just too easy to make a quick choice—snap, send, share—and it's gone.

It's hard to nail down the hard data on sexting, because most of the reports released recently contain data collected three to five years ago. And we all know from our experiences as parents and in our communities that in the last two or three years, there has been an explosion in smartphone ownership and usage. And with that, there's been a large effort to strengthen the education and communication on sexting.

The FBI uses this definition for sexting: "sending or receiving sexually explicit or sexually suggestive nude or seminude images or video, generally via cell phone." Like cyberbullying, sexting is relatively new in our social culture. Law enforcement, school districts, and families are all trying to navigate codes of conduct and the consequences for those who engage in it—particularly minors—and to develop appropriate awareness campaigns. For now, the most crucial step we can take in our own homes to prevent sexting is running an awareness campaign of our own. Talk to your kids about sexting and stand behind what you say.

Say This about Sexting!

- If you receive or send a picture of a sexual nature, please let me know. I can help you handle it. Even if it's awkward, I love you unconditionally. We can figure it out together.
- Never forward a sexual picture you receive.
- Block or delete a contact that makes you uncomfortable. You don't have to be friends or followers with everyone online.

○ It's not just scary, it's the truth: Sharing sexual pictures of under-age people is against the law. Even if it's your friend from history class or a person you've never met.

○ If you find sexting hard to resist, think of the person you respect or admire the most. Ask yourself this before you send a pic: *What would that very special person think if they saw this?* Let that be your guide when you feel confused or have the impulse to share a picture. If you cannot find strategies to stop yourself from send-ing or receiving sext messages, ask an adult you trust for guidance.

○ No one that truly cares about you will ask for a picture that you don't want to send. Never forget that!

○ Sharing, spreading, or requesting sexts does not make you more appealing, cooler, or more likely to be included among your peers. Your social status will be increased by making positive decisions.

○ The thrill of sexting will not last. It is not private. You can pre-vent a lot of chaos and unwanted feelings in your life if you just avoid it.

I've heard some stories that might make you squirm. For example, when she was in college, Jamie sent a topless photo of herself to her boyfriend, Joey. Without her knowledge, Joey shared it with the entire men's soccer team. The teammates all saved the photo and continued to pass it on to new people. Today, three years after graduating from col-lege, Jamie is a working professional. At an after-work social event she bumps into one of her peers from college. He laughs and casually says, "I still have that pic of you Joey sent us saved on my phone." She is horri-fied, embarrassed, and furious. The relationship has long since ended, but her privacy and trust continue to be violated. She cannot imagine how many people her picture has reached. She feels helpless—mad at herself and mad at Joey—but has to live with this choice she made on an impulse, deeming it "harmless" during college.

I Found a Nudie Pic—HELP!

Depending on whether your child is the sender or receiver, be prepared to ask some version of these questions.

O Why do you have this picture?

O Why did you send this picture?

O Do you have permission to have this picture?

O Was it sent directly to you by the person in the picture?

O Have you forwarded or shared this picture with anyone else?

O Were you pressured to send this picture?

Call a meeting with your child.

O Create a space of trust, safety, and privacy.

O Ask the above questions. Get the story.

O If what you learn indicates that this is case of abuse or misuse, take immediate action: Take the phone or device away, inform law enforcement officials if necessary (when it involves minors communicating with adults, strangers, force or coercion, bribery, cyberbullying), and if you feel overwhelmed, seek professional advice and guidance.

O If you learn that the matter involves consenting peers, assess what needs to be done. Depending on the exact circumstances, you might delete the pictures, ask for or make an apology, have a conversation with the other child's family, and/or discuss the risks and consequences with your child.

When Kari was in college, she and some friends took some sexual photos of themselves while partying and saved them on her phone. It was wild but harmless fun. What could possibly go wrong? Well, Kari left her phone in a dressing room soon after. The next day, she reported the loss to the staff at the shop in the hope that the phone would turn up, and then she carried on with her afternoon. In the meantime, a patron of the store found her phone and of course accessed the sexual pictures on it. The woman decided to share the sexual pictures to Kari's social networking accounts using the upload app installed on the phone. Kari's friends and family (yes, aunts, grandparents, nephew) panicked and started calling her, but obviously she was not reachable by phone. Eventually, some friends caught up with her and told her what had happened, and she quickly logged in on her laptop to delete them from her pages. But the damage was already done. Her phone was never found, and more than a year later, Kari still worries that the pictures will be shared again or will turn up somewhere unexpectedly.

A thirteen-year-old, Sadie, sent a Snapchat picture of herself wearing a thong to a boy she liked in her class. Snapchat photos self-destruct in under ten seconds, so she didn't think about it much. This boy took a screenshot of the picture and saved it on his phone— which meant he was in possession of this picture forever, even though that was not Sadie's intention, and he could do whatever he pleased with it. And being a thirteen-year-old himself, he decided to share it with all of his friends.

Sam is eleven years old. One day he decided to take a video of himself. He was wearing shorts with no shirt and was staring straight into the mirror, flexing his muscles, posing, and grunting. He uploaded it to YouTube and texted a few girls the link to watch it. Word traveled that Sam, who struggles socially, did this. Without Sam knowing how fast it spread, everyone was getting laughs out of his attempt to impress. Because Sam wasn't part of certain social circles, he didn't realize the impact of and ridicule generated by this one video. All of the likes and comments that read "awesome" were sarcastic, but that was lost on Sam. Two years later, kids still parody and mock Sam and the video.

Ken likes a girl in his sophomore class named Jenna. They've known each other for a long time. Their mothers have known each other since they were waitresses together during the kids' preschool years. Ken has recently become interested in Jenna romantically and they've been talking more and more. One night Jenna asks Ken what he's doing. Ken sends a "dick pic," a picture of his erect penis, to Jenna. Jenna immediately screams and, embarrassed and horrified, runs to her mother. Jenna's mom calls Ken's mom and explains the situation. All of this happens within minutes—the picture, Jenna's surprise, the mothers' involvement. Ken's mother runs up the stairs yelling for Ken to explain himself. He locks himself in his bedroom, certain he can never show his face anywhere again. The impacts of the impulsive decision to take and send the picture, no doubt driven by adolescent hormones, will stay with Ken for a long time, damaging not only his reputation, but also any chance he might have at seriously dating Jenna.

Truth: I did not think that I would ever author a book with the words "dick pic" in it. But here we are. You, fine reader, deserve to know even the most ridiculous slang.

iRule Tip: Tell your child that there should never be a time or situation when they feel so lost, embarrassed, or ashamed that they cannot come to you. Every mistake or problem can be dealt with if communicated. Please be certain that your child knows you understand the risks of online use and that you are there for them no matter what. They need to see you as a person they can turn to if they lose their way and find trouble while using technology.

PART 3

Live Fully

Have fun, play, go outside, be silly, be willing to make mistakes, create, imagine, be curious, seek, serve, give back.

○ ○ ●

Be Present

iRule: Pictures

> **My iRule:** Don't take a zillion pictures and videos. There is no need to document everything. Live your experiences. They will be stored in your memory for eternity.

Stop for a minute. Think about the last time you reached for your phone to take a picture. Think about what it was you captured, how important the photo is to you, and how you used it. With smartphones, picture taking can involve a lot more than just pointing and clicking. We often keep our heads down for minutes cropping, editing, uploading, captioning, and sharing photos. Was that last picture you took worth it? I hope so. Earlier in this book, we talked about picture taking and sharing, preventing "friend fails," and asking for "Permission to Post!" We talked about picture taking and sharing in reference to selfies, nudies, and sexting. But there's more to say. I know this is a book about raising kids in this age of technology, but I have to start somewhere. And at some point, the conversation needs to find its way to us.

I think one of the most popular uses of the technology involves photos—taking them, sharing them, and struggling to parent them now in a fast and furious modern world. So let's deepen the conversation and talk about our own common behaviors before we look more closely at our kids and their usage. I do it. I overdo it. I'm sure you do it

 # How to Resist the Pic and Other Slow Tech Camera Phone Awareness Tips

○ Heading out with the kids? Leave your phone behind—in the car, at home, or off or set to DO NOT DISTURB in your pocket.

○ Ask yourself, "Do I need this picture?" Is it necessary for my co-workers and childhood classmates, my mother's friends, and my uncles to see this picture? Or is it something I could text about to the people for whom it is intended?

○ Consciously make yourself pause. Take a breath. Just wait, see if the urge to text, check, scroll, take a picture is still there.

○ Question why you're taking this picture. To preserve a memory? To post or text to friends? Because it's funny or wild or different? Because you're bored?

too. Pictures—here, there, and everywhere. As parents today, we are force-fed so much about "being present," "living in the moment," "they're only little once," the anxiety could stop our hearts. I live this. I think this is part of the reason I write so much about parenting, because I'm trying so damn hard to hold on to something that cannot be held—time, growth, life. But what does it mean to really be present for ourselves and for the people we love? I think it means setting personal and professional boundaries. I think it means being in one place at a time—not at a soccer game texting about an upcoming meeting.

O Consider what message you'll send or how it will present you if you share the picture. Fun? Wild? Crazy? Serious? Artsy? Sexy? Good? Responsible? Engaged?

O What reaction do you hope to get from sharing this picture? Likes? Comments? Inside jokes? Anger? Approval? Sometimes it's enough to take a picture and keep it for yourself. Not every moment needs to be shared.

O Consider whether picture sharing might be a habit for you. Do you need to document and share everything? Can having the experience be enough on its own?

O Chill out. Seriously, I know it's overstated, but not oversimplified here. Just have a picnic or a run or a morning at the playground or a night out with friends. That's it. Just have that. No proof, no posting. Enjoy.

Not eating dinner and scrolling Facebook. It means saying no sometimes—to work, to kids, to partners, to neighbors, to family, to perfection. It means deliberately carving out time to do things that have real value to you. And it all takes practice.

As I continue to evolve as a mother and woman, I'm starting to see that when I'm truly present in the moment, there is no space or reason for me to reach for my phone or my camera. I used to think it helped me preserve what is precious. I believed it was a gift to constantly be connected to everyone. But what it often does is take me right out of living those moments. Sometimes the urge to capture or connect is so intense I have to use strategies to help myself let it go. I'll say in my head, *Just be here* or *Stay still,* and it helps me stay engaged. These tools of attention and awareness bring me back to my parenting intentions.

There are also moments when I want to be having more fun than I am. I want it to look like a full-blown, grand, exciting adventure. But it's just not. And that's okay too; I don't need to force the fun either. I owe it to myself to hang in there and make the best of it or call it a day. Either way, there is no perfect lighting, pose, or scenery, there are no perfect people or perfect martinis that can make something fun when it's moderately or totally not fun—even if you take a great picture. Okay, perfect martinis can enhance the fun, but it's usually temporary.

So yes, this iRule arose from my own habit of constantly documenting moments with pictures—especially now that camera technology has made it so easy and portable. I find myself taking pictures of a beautiful salad or perfectly brewed latte; my kids on the swings, at bat, at school; my new sneakers; a sunset during a beach run—everything! I see this in my own peers too. Every day our kids are used as photo subjects to the point that we sometimes pass up on living the moment to capture it.

I am actually ashamed to admit that I have even taken my children out of living in the moment to take their picture. That's right, I said it. I have begged, bribed, coerced, and occasionally yelled at my kids to stop what they were doing so I could snap a photo: "Look up and smile!" "Hug your sister and pose!" or "Stop it—cooperate!" And I imagine their brilliant little minds thinking, "You cooperate; we were happily digging in the sand!" Just like you, I love my kids. I think they are insanely cute. They do amazing and adorable things every day—millions of times a day! And there's so many of them and they have so many interests that the picture-taking possibilities are literally limitless—Ella rides a horse! Cassidy plays with a friend! Greg is up to bat! Brendan gets new shoes! Lily does a split! And I guess that's what has stopped me, that word "limitless." When will it be enough? What isn't worthy of capturing? How do I trust enough to know that experiences alone will satisfy me?

See, here's the thing. I was a mother from 1999 to 2009 without a camera phone. I managed. I have a lot of pictures from those days. I even have printed copies in actual photo albums as proof! Because let's face it, there are moments in parenthood we must capture. It's part of our DNA and our history—holidays, first days of school, newborn babies swaddled in hospital blankets, weddings, parties, pets, performances, vacations. And I have all of those pictures! Then I have some pictures from incidents here and there—an afternoon when Brendan and Greg were little that show them jumping in and out of the plastic backyard pool, and when I bought them matching baby blue pajamas and they posed in them just out of the bath. I love those pictures. I remember the events. Then there're some silly ones of Ella as a baby wearing my sunglasses or eating corn on the cob for the first time. What I don't have is their entire early childhoods documented. I can measure the difference in Cassidy (born in 2007) compared to her older siblings since I probably have at least a picture a day of her—on the swings, at the coffee shop, with her friends, in a costume, on a walk, playing with a new toy, eating ice cream, laying on the couch under a blanket, reading a book at the library. I call her early life with me "the iPhone years" because I texted, e-mailed, posted, and connected on most of my days with her.

I actually have spent a lot of time trying to remember how I interacted with my children, with my extended family and friends, when taking and sharing pictures wasn't so central to our lives. I think I just took pictures when I felt inclined and most of the time I didn't. Instead of taking a picture of Gregory picking apples on his preschool field trip and sending it to his grandparents in real time, I picked an apple too. Then I sat down with him and ate it. I probably even watched him eat it, bite after bite (because that's what you do with firstborns) and chatted with the people around me instead of cropping, editing, and uploading with my head down. And I know I sound like I'm being harsh—on myself and on the culture—but it's not judgment. I love all of the pictures I have of the kids. Each one tells a story, and I'm so grateful for my camera phone's ease of use and for having the ability to share the pictures. I really am. But there were points when taking a picture became the point. And when I became aware of that, I knew I needed to change. So I tried something that took some courage. I started leaving my phone—my camera—behind.

As you can imagine, my awareness of my own behaviors heightened when I decided to give Gregory his iPhone. When I started to formulate his iRules in my mind, I had to ask myself why there was such a difference between what I wanted for him and the expectations I had for myself. Why did I insist that he not "document everything" while I did? I had to look at my habits and behaviors with the technology. So I started practicing. I remember deliberately leaving my phone in the car during a family hike last fall, and then I paid attention to what changed. First of all, there were no struggles with the kids about posing or waiting or holding still so I could get a picture. Second, I just walked along, talking or not, and watched the kids. Additionally, I didn't worry that my phone was going to drop, break, ring, buzz, or run out of battery power. Naturally, there were moments—like when they all climbed the leaning tree at once—when I wished I had my camera. Instead, I just sat on a log and waited.

Do you know how many years I have longed to sit down and wait? There were days when even imagining a moment when the kids could play and explore while I *sat down* was impossible. People! When Brendan and Ella were toddlers, I chased after them up into a tree house, one hand flailing in the air to block them from falling and the other one squeezing newborn Lily against me while she was breastfeeding. Yes, I climbed a giant ladder to a tree house, panicked and sweating, while breastfeeding a newborn. And now, when everyone finally has some independence, I'm going to chase after them with a camera so I don't miss a moment of it? What the hell is wrong with me? Have I lost my mind? Sit on the log, Janell. Sit on a log and smile about having gotten this far.

So yes, on that hike, it was a relief to be without my camera. I hadn't expected that. I hadn't realized how much of my mental space having my phone with me had occupied. I didn't know that it was distracting me, actually taking me away from the moment, instead of bringing me closer to it. So I started doing it more—leaving my phone home, off, or put away when we went to the beach, school plays (gasp!), on neighborhood walks, at restaurants and family events. And guess what? I never regretted it! I actually prefer to be with the kids without my camera. It suits me and has carried over to moments when I am not with them too. When I'm with friends or enjoying a dinner with my mom and sisters, I just don't want to use it. The fewer pictures I take, the less I feel the pull to take them.

And now that I have a little distance from overusing my camera, I can see how much space and meaning the devices have for others. I watch them dig their phones out of their bags and try to get the best shot or the best one million shots of something funny or a "can't miss" pic. Now listen, I really do love picture sharing and social networking. I am a social being, an extrovert, a lover of people. I love seeing photos of my college friend's little babies. I love seeing how much my neighbor's daughter has grown. I love the sunset on Martha's Vineyard that my son's teacher posted. I love to see all the families I know enjoying their time together having ice cream or bonfires or baseball games. I love the smiles on my friends' faces at the finish lines of races, on date nights, at celebrations, and I even love #tbt (Throwback Thursday) pics.

I think this is a really special time to be alive. I think we get to know people in our communities better because we see their statuses—from personal and political to serious and silly. We learn about a neighbor having lost their dad to cancer ten years ago, or that they're passionate and want to raise awareness about a cause. I wouldn't learn these things when we say hello at the grocery store or at an open house once a year. We get to go beyond having just baseline knowledge about people: father of three, works at the hospital, lives on Sunny Lane. We deepen our knowledge and connections and build relationships from there. That is special.

Technology helps us stay in touch with our roots—old neighbors, extended family members, teammates, teachers. I see pictures of Adam's cousin traveling all over the world and read about my college friend leaving her successful career to stay home with her daughters. I get to see these experiences unfold and feel like a part of them. It bridges distance for families and friends spread throughout the world. When we do visit in person, we can talk about tangible, real-time happenings we've been watching develop online. We feel caught up and the relationship can continue to expand.

I believe that this is how our children feel too. They get to know their peers beyond what they see in the classroom or in the cafeteria. A girl sees a song lyric quoted by a classmate she had math with, she retweets it, and they build a connection. A boy sees a picture of the family of a kid he knows from across town and they realize their little siblings are really good friends. Someone has a sick grandfather, someone else an exciting vacation, someone else lost a close game. We can feel compassion or disappointment or joy right along with them. That is a beautiful piece of social networking to understand: Our children care about what's happening with their peers—good and bad—just like we do. Where do caring and taking an interest balance with obsessing and FOMO (fear of missing out)? The answer will feel different for each family. I think about the ways you keep in balance socially online and model that for your children.

Note: *This is exactly what Adam hates about social networking—the people. And sorry to everyone we know that this may offend. He only used it to promote and share his music. How boring is he? When he stepped back from playing music so much, he found absolutely no need for Facebook or Twitter or anything else online. He's introverted and more private than me. So I'll just share all of our secrets for him. And he'll be in touch with you only when he expects to see you at his concerts. Sound good?*

And then there's this piece of picture taking that I have to dig into, that I have to address. Sometimes we take pictures of our lives just so we can share them online. And that's okay. Admitting is the first step. But my take is this: Post and share photos with intention. If you are with people you love or having a blast, share away, because that is authentic and real. Those pictures have a voice, a message. But if you are forcing the fun and trying too hard, skip the sharing and just be present in your own mediocre life like the rest of us.

This is a great perspective to teach our children too. Here's a little secret of being human: We don't need to take pictures every time we are together to have fun. We don't need to share the pictures every time we are together to have fun. We can just have fun and nobody may ever know about it. And to take this point even further, we don't even need to have fun every time we are with friends. That's not realistic. Some days, some activities, some outings are naturally going to be better than others. Let that be okay for our children. Tell them this. Tell them the fun is not in the numbers of comments and likes or the amount of attention a picture receives. The fun is not always meant to be shared. The fun can be personal or private and still have as much meaning as it does when it is posted.

The Camera Phone Generation

We live in a neighborhood rich with children and families. It is safe. It has space. Families welcome children. Multiage play is encouraged. It's a great place to grow up. This neighborhood is one of my most cherished aspects of raising children. When Greg and his buddies were in sixth grade, a lot of the boys started to get their own phones. This was new and sudden. I felt like this group of kids—what they liked and how they played—had been abruptly invaded. Normally, I never tended to them. I hardly even peeked out the window to see if they were in one piece. They traveled in packs, going from lawn to lawn in all kinds of weather, all year long. They wanted to be outside forming pickup games in every sport's season and they wanted to be left alone. They solved problems and were generally good to each other, so they had all the freedom and independence that goes with that. But on one particular day, they started a basketball game. It would start and stop. They were wandering in and out of the house. It was quieter than usual. I went outside and saw at least five of the boys sitting on the lawn, slouched over their cell phones. I watched. Passing around the phones, they showed videos or texts or pictures to each other. They laughed a little. But more than anything, this great big playground that had existed for these kids for years suddenly shrank to the size of a private, handheld device. I felt they were being robbed of their childhood. Seriously, I felt that extreme. It really disturbed me. They were eleven and twelve, prime ages for active, self-directed play. But instead, they were giving it up, sacrificing it. With the ever-more-widespread use of cell phones, I knew this was a slowly closing chapter.

And it continued; the cell phones became central to their time together. Even when they did play, they started taking pictures and videos of the games. The kids sitting out stared at their phones instead of chatting with the other kids waiting to sub in. And that's harmless. Really, I know. I could be worrying about so much more. They could be drinking or stealing or shooting up or whatever some kids do, somewhere. But I watched the transition—it was tangible. I watched the cell phones come into their lives and the free play leave. I watched the point of the playing become documenting it. Who had the best dunk? Who hit a sweet outside jumper? Who took it to the hoop on whom? Who should post or send the picture or video? And I had to ask myself if they were just growing up. Did I reach an age when I stopped making dance routines with the neighbors in the backyard and started talking on the phone all afternoon instead? Probably. And this is obvious and maybe even nostalgic, but my giant cordless phone couldn't fit into my pocket or make calls from my neighbor's tree fort. So even if most of the time I thought I was too cool to dabble in child's play as a tween, I did it anyway. And I was fully present.

A Story about Being Present

Last summer Adam and I were going through a particularly chaotic time together. I was working full-time running a high-intensity, wildly fun summer camp and writing this book. He was working full-time and training for a huge bucket-list race. We were raising our family, running the house, and picking up all of the pieces that result in living in sheer chaos. We weren't connecting. I was going to sleep when the kids did and waking up before the sun. He was working out, getting the kids out the door to meet me at camp, and putting in full days at the office. Our weekends were crammed with commitments—deadlines, family gatherings, birthday parties, baseball tournaments, and laundry—a lot of laundry.

One steamy late-summer Saturday, fried and bordering on broken, we needed some family time. See, I always tell people you can measure the state of my mental health by the size of the laundry pile in the mudroom. When the laundry pile is low, I'm feeling in tune, efficient, and organized. When it's taller than I am, I'm burning the candle at both ends and everyone else around here likely is too. On this day, I'm pretty sure it was sky-high. Adam and I are the kind of couple (and we are the kind of family) that needs to physically see each other to be high functioning. We like to process, commiserate about, plan, assess, and dissect all things. When this slips, so do we. I had also been observing the kids and seeing increased junk food consumption, fresh behavior, weird sleep patterns from late nights, and a general buzzing. We needed each other, a reset amid the wildness. It was midafternoon by the time we got our plan in motion, so we decided to pack dinner and head to a beach "down Cape." We only get to Mayflower Beach once a summer or so because it's a good drive from our house, not across town like our everyday (though equally as special) beaches.

The kids are whining and fighting. Adam and I aren't really talking, we're working, trying very hard to pull a little adventure together on limited energy and patience. I want to sleep on the drive, but I sit up, knowing I should use this car ride to catch up with Adam. He's quiet, annoyed that I pushed so hard for this and the kids don't even want to go. We arrive and agree to leave our phones in the car, since our goal is to recharge.

Leaving phones behind continues to be easier for my thirteen-year-old than it is for me. Greg looks at me and says, "Mom, I left it at home. I knew I wouldn't need it here." Thanks for the life lesson, G. Sometimes I think I made the iRules contract for myself.

We head out to the beach. It is a gorgeous afternoon. It's low tide and the soft sand stretches out for miles. The water is warm and calm with perfect waves. We set up quickly and all of us hustle into the ocean. The water literally melts me. Shamefully, I haven't been in the ocean all season. I can feel what I carry pull away. I feel free. We swim. We eat. The girls dig and build. Brendan joins them. When Greg's around, Brendan tends to ditch the girls, but today there is space and time and even a little bit of peace. To watch an eleven-year-old boy shed his cool, take a lime-green shovel, and play in the sand for close to an hour is as close to heaven on earth as I can imagine. We throw footballs and Frisbees. We sit and enjoy snacks and the salty breeze. We all let go a little. We've been at this for hours and soon the sun starts to leave. We do a last call for swimming and dive in. Lying in the ocean, we watch the sky overhead go from yellow to deep orange to vibrant pink and purple as the sun drops. It is as divine as it sounds. As I lie there, watching the day end, the girls letting the waves carry them to shore, the boys begging to stay, I wish I could bottle it. Absurdly, I think about my iPhone, my camera, and in what ways I would try to capture this moment if I could. I realize there is no way. Today, the only way is living.

We pack up and pile into the car. Brendan tells me he's never seen me swim so much. He is giddy. Ella says it was her favorite day of summer. She is content. They all ask if we can come back to this beach again tomorrow or next weekend. They want more of what we had today. There is a calm over us. Yes, it was the beach, it was the weather, it was the timing. But more than anything, everything that happened in those five hours at the beach happened because all seven of us were present.

I share this story with other women and families that I know. I hear the same sentiment expressed. One friend reflects on her family's trip to a water park. She asked herself, "Why was that so fun?" And the only clear answer was that neither she nor her husband brought their cell phones. She felt like they checked out for the day and were truly present with their family. Another mom I know said she was so tired of hearing her daughter say, "Can you put your phone away?" that she only uses social networking sites when her daughter is napping or in bed for the night. She said it has made their days happier and less difficult.

This idea is confirmed for me again and again as I talk to families.

Whenever we are taken away from the present moment, we lose our footing. So I know this about my family: When we are struggling, it is

 ## How We Stay Present

- We schedule regular stretches of free time away from technology. Daily—at meals and school and before bed. Weekly—on hikes, family visits, and beach walks (even in the winter).

- We talk. A lot. My favorite time of the day is when we hang around our kitchen island catching up with the kids about their day, laughing or sharing stories together. Our real-time family is way better than any social networking site!

- We hold each other accountable. If someone is buried in the technology, we speak up. The kids will even say to me, "Mom, eyes up! I was asking you something" if I'm head down, texting.

- No-fuss tech time. On weekend mornings the kids can go for it—iPad, Xbox, phone. We don't breathe down their necks when it's open time and they can just enjoy some technology. This helps keep the tech from invading other parts of our lives when they have some time to self-monitor and self-regulate.

- We turn our phones off or to silent or DO NOT DISTURB if we know the temptation will be too great.

- We love many things—sports, nature, art, music, books, dancing, people. This keeps us alive and engaged.

often because some (or all) of us are not living in the moment. We aren't present. We're hurried or worrying or planning or over-whelmed about the past or the future or distracted right now. When we get into this frazzled space, I know the technology needs to take a seat in the way back of our lives, and carving out that space helps all of us. When you're creating your family's iRules, you may want to be prepared for the present by setting some guidelines on what it means to be present too.

The Critics

This iRules contract point received some negative feedback when I shared it publicly. I was asked why I would stifle my son's creativity by limiting what he chooses to capture. For me, this point goes along with the attachment to technology. A professional photographer whose family has attended my parenting workshops takes pictures in developing countries. He tells me that his camera is his barrier. It sepa-rates him from the subject and scene. Professionally, this allows him to photograph intense or traumatic scenes, like when he traveled to Haiti after the earthquake. But it also has the same effect in our everyday lives. When we are busy filming every move, we are building a barrier between ourselves and the experience. We take ourselves out of living In the moment. The truth is that not every moment is worth capturing. Being present is far more important and valuable.

So ask yourself, *How does my child use and share pictures and videos?* Is she out photographing the leaves changing on a fall afternoon, then editing the shots and sharing them online? Or is she squeezing sun-block on her cleavage with her tongue sticking out? I'm serious! I have seen both kinds of photos taken by teens that are the exact same age. I think it should be pretty clear which one you should be encouraging because it is healthy, artistic expression and which one you should be discouraging by confiscating the phone until more appropriate behaviors are demonstrated. Is your son wrapped in a towel and flex-ing in the mirror? Greg tried this once and within seconds took the pic down from Instagram because he felt "weird" about it. Um, yeah. Because it is weird. You're twelve. Go climb a tree or tease your sisters or something. Or is your son making videos of comedy movies he wrote with his friends and sharing them on YouTube? Greg also tried this. I loved it. We bought him moviemaking software and let them jump around the house for hours wearing size 5T superhero costumes and wrestling. Even though it was absurd, I saw real value in their act-ing and creativity. I saw it as a big-kid version of play. And making the videos just supported it.

☑ **iRule Tip:** Teach your child not to live through a lens. Not every moment is worth documenting. Show your child the differences among recording a moment of a special occasion, having some fun with the camera, and obsessive or distracted picture taking.

iRule: FOMO (Fear of Missing Out)

My iRule: Leave your phone home sometimes and feel safe and secure making that decision. It is not alive or an extension of you. Learn to live without it. Be bigger and more powerful than FOMO (fear of missing out).

When we live like we might miss something or live like everyone else is having all of the fun, we rob ourselves of actually enjoying or being present right where we are. I love the expression "standing knee deep in a river dying of thirst." I can't remember where I first read it, but as it turns out, it's a country song recorded by Kathy Mattea in the early '90s. I use it as a personal mantra and also as a lesson to my family. When I (or we) feel someone has something or is doing something that we want to have or do, I come back to this lesson on abundance and gratitude. It allows me to stop for a moment and think, *What do I have right here with me that is beautiful and amazing?* or *What experiences am I having that are special?* Often we don't see our own lives as sacred or important; instead, we focus on the idea that everyone else has it all.

Technology has heightened that impression for our entire family. Brendan can see who gets to stay up later than him to play Xbox Live because their names are listed on the screen. Ella knows her neighborhood friends get to text their cousins because they have iPod Touches and she doesn't. We are inundated with other people's photos. It seems as if everyone is constantly upgrading phones and video game systems, and the expectation becomes automatic: "I want that!" I like to use a tool I call the pause. The pause can be silence, waiting, or delaying. It can be as simple as taking a deep breath before speaking, getting a good night's sleep before responding to an e-mail, or something larger, like delaying the use of a specific technology. In taking this pause, we hope for reflection and patience. We hope to be more deliberate with our choices.

I can remember when all of Greg's peers started to get flip phones, when he was about ten years old or so. It happened suddenly. The more friends that got phones, the more urgent it felt to him to have one. Greg pushed for one. I couldn't see the need. I was home most of the time with the girls, Adam works right down the road, everywhere Greg went he knew people. It wasn't practical. Beyond the lack of a need for it, I didn't want to parent it. I was up to my eyeballs in raising little kids and I didn't want to step into adolescent waters before our

Parenting the Pause

○ Teach your children to breathe. Tell them to take a lot of big, deep breaths regularly. It will calm their nervous systems and allow them to be present in their bodies before taking an action, even if it's just for a moment.

○ Teach them to be aware of their bodies. *Relax your jaw. Unclench your fists. Let your shoulders come down.* These are some of the places where all of us hold tension. We can let some of that go.

○ Encourage your kids to wait until the next sunrise to respond to an online conversation that is bothering them or is uncomfortable (excluding issues of safety and legality). Show them that some issues feel urgent and if we respond impulsively, we may regret it later. Sometimes a response is never necessary. Sometimes a response is required, but time. It felt important to practice the pause. Adam and I agreed to delay it. Greg pleaded some more, and we talked with him about what was behind his need to have one. Did he feel left out? Was he bored? How would he use it? Who would he text or call? In this case, delaying Greg's acquisition of a cell phone helped him to appreciate the one he finally received at age thirteen. With growth and maturity, he understood that having one is a privilege because he had learned to live without one. He knew that we could take it away as quickly as we gave it to him, so abusing it would never work to his benefit.

But it takes courage to use the pause in all aspects of life. We are so quick to answer, to know, to have, that we don't question enough. It's not very often that we take the time to think through our choices— or even remember that we do have choices! It may feel like you need

giving it mindful attention when our emotions have cooled and are clearer forces us to make better choices with our words and intentions.

○ Wait! Wait for an Instagram account. Wait for a cell phone. Wait for the latest video game system. It helps our children be clear on what we really want and makes it that much sweeter when they finally do get it.

○ Teach your children to ask themselves questions. *Do I want to share this picture? Why? What is the point of making this joke online? Will my friends know I'm joking? Who will likely see this if I share it?*

○ Accept and welcome silence. Let it be quiet—in their minds, in their rooms, during car rides, at the table. There is so much static; teach them to unwind their minds.

to provide a specific video game system, smartphone, e-reader, or music device for your child because everyone has one and it's become the norm. That is parenting from fear: fear that your child might be left out, left behind, or have to make do. Just because it seems that all the children have personal devices doesn't mean that it's the right time or action for your family. Use the pause. Think about the impact it will have on the whole family. Think about the boundaries or iRules you will need to set and then enforce. Think about your child's age and degree of personal development.

Because Greg received his smartphone at thirteen, Brendan and Ella are now counting the days until they're thirteen, when they can have their very own. It doesn't work like that. We agree that around age thirteen is when we will start the conversation about a phone. It does not guarantee that each child will get one then. We have to assess each child. Obviously, their needs and behaviors will vary. What's happening for our family will also vary at different points in time. Perhaps Adam or I are traveling for work more than usual and the family system is taxed. That would not be a great time to give a new iPhone to one of the kids just because they are thirteen. I want to be fully present, to teach them how to have healthy tech habits and behaviors. There is a lot to consider; making quick, poorly thought out decisions related to technology can lead to regret or struggles when we haven't properly prepared our expectations about or boundaries for its use. Leave some space, use the pause, think about it. Talk to your kids and your partner about the technology. Agree to buy or introduce it when you feel ready.

We apply this to other areas of life. If the kids want to try out for a sport as a member of what we call a "travel" team, meaning one that plays teams from throughout the state, then they need to wait until fifth grade. Fifth grade seemed like a good age for the kids to decide what they really liked, so our family could put a little more time and money into an activity or sport that really excited them. We also felt like they could jump in a carpool and look after themselves more independently at that age. That's our family rule. However, when Brendan showed a knack and passion for soccer during third grade and offered to give up baseball and any other spring activity to play, we reassessed our family guidelines and made an exception. Just like our iRules on technology, we follow family guidelines that are flexible and consider many factors.

A few years ago my boys wanted an Xbox 360. We had a Nintendo Wii and years' worth of games and equipment for it. I couldn't imagine having two game systems and starting our collection over. But the boys wouldn't let it go. So Adam and I decided that if the boys really wanted an Xbox 360, they would need to sell their Wii console and games and pay for the difference. We knew my in-laws were potential buyers because they wanted a Wii at their house, but the boys didn't have access to this insider info. I was determined to make this process at least a little bit of a challenge for them. First, I wanted them to see and appreciate the value and understand how much things cost. Obviously, selling all of their Wii games would only cover the purchase of one or two new Xbox games, so they also had to consider that their huge game collection was about to shrink substantially. Second, I wanted to make sure they wouldn't be looking to upgrade every time something new came out. I wanted to teach them to appreciate and enjoy what they had.

So the boys spent a day taking inventory of their goodies and collecting data on the used Wii's market value. They typed up a package for purchase and started pitching it to people. Luckily for them, they scored a meeting with my in-laws and closed the deal. Within a few weeks they had a brand-new Xbox and a game or two. This is an example of using the pause. Of course my in-laws would have been willing to give them the money up front without all the details, but we wanted it to be a process. I wanted the boys fully invested in the decision making. I wanted them to see and understand that we don't just throw away, upgrade, or move on when something new comes out. This may seem like a small thing, but I consider it one of my great parenting victories because we took the time to see this through, enforcing our expectations and our family values on stuff. I really believe our boys learned a lot. They both talk about the "Wii sale" experience to this day.

As I explore all the ways our children can feel that they are missing out when technology and online communication play a central role in their lives, I have to go deeper, past the technology, to what it represents. If a friend gets a pair of expensive shoes and posts a pic, how does your child feel? If a Facebook friend's life "seems" or "looks" better or more interesting than their own, what emotions does your child experience? It is our job to preserve their sense of self, their sense of gratitude. Can our children be happy about their peers' successes, possessions, experiences, and still feel happy about themselves? Or do they shut down and experience self-pity? Ask them how seeing what is posted online makes them feel. Notice their tone, the energy, what isn't said when they reference their friends' lives online. We can take deliberate steps to be certain that our children feel a deep sense of appreciation for their lives, so that their centers are not rocked by what happens to their peers. We must create a space for them to return to and connect with inside our homes and inside their beings.

Appreciate the Life You're Living— Your Kids Will Too!

O Gratitude is contagious. Be thankful for it all.

O Keep a daily or weekly gratitude journal. List the ordinary and the amazing—matching socks, car repairs, a healthy baby, a pay raise.

O Constantly praise the people around you. Every day. "Isn't Mrs. Jordan so generous? She took the time to make pizza with all of you."

○ Tell your kids how awesome your home is (even if you hate the paint color or the crusty old windows). Literally, list how it benefits your family: "I'm so glad that one of the bedrooms in our house is oversized so that all three girls fit perfectly!"

○ Praise your community, schools, region. "I can't believe we are lucky enough to live in a place that people from all over the world visit." Doesn't that sound so much better than "I hate this tourist traffic!"?

○ Go outside. Point out the leaves changing, the tides, the moon cycle, a flower blooming, a tomato in the garden. Let yourself be in awe of nature. It will connect your kids to something deeper.

○ Set goals. Having a vision for future experiences will help classify wants in the "this will happen to me" category instead of the "this happens to everyone else" category. Ask the kids where they want to visit, what they want to study, where they want to live someday. Suddenly, it will all seem possible.

When I Was Young . . .

Go on, gather the kids and tell that story! Remember what it felt like to be a child—describe your neighborhood, your city block, your beaches, meadows, or playgrounds. Talk about the freedom you had to explore and express yourself. The more connected we are to our childhood innocence and bliss, the greater the motivation is to provide it for our own children. This is something that all families can do. Most of you probably already share pieces of your story. The conversation can be weaved into the corners and kitchen tables and car rides of our lives.

But how does it relate to technology? What impact does storytelling or sharing have on the ways in which our children use technology? Well, first, it takes time. To tell or hear a story, you need to have the time and space to do so. You need to look at each other and listen. You need experiences to relate to your own life and to be in tune and present when your children want or need to hear them. You need to be open, willing to share and receive stories in return. You need to be temporarily free of distractions. I think that storytelling helps children and teens see their parents as people. Real people with ups and downs, successes and failures.

I think storytelling highlights our priorities, what's important to us, what we've learned. It forces us to reflect. Even if I heard a story that didn't directly relate to my life experiences, I felt that story. I also have this weird parenting thing I do to myself: I try to imagine what my kids will say about certain days or moments of their lives when they are grown. I think perhaps because I am a writer and I enjoy narrative, I like to imagine their grown-up memoirs. This can be a trap sometimes, mostly because just about everything I do is flawed and I can be a total beast of a human being. Inner dialogue: *Holy crap, they will tell the entire world I said and did things that made them unhappy and made me unhappy and a lot of the time we were unhappy with each other.* But most of the time, because I am doing my very best at motherhood, it is not a trap. It is wonderful. I think about them remembering as adults how they grew up by the ocean, how they were raised on the tides. They'll tell their children, their readers, their students, their citizens that at high tide you could jump the boardwalk, float in the creek, and drop in a kayak with ease. At low tide you could run along the soft sand beaches out to the sandbars, go crabbing, or explore along the grassy, muddy, earthy creek bank for miles.

In my mind I have taken a snapshot for them of the many days that have become one in the story of their lives. It goes like this: A large group of boys, maybe ten to fifteen years old, stands along the edge of the marsh, divided into teams. They have grown out of their sand toys, grown out of Goldfish and juice boxes on a blanket, they are growing right out of their bodies. Some of them are brothers or neighbors or classmates, some of them brought cousins or new kids or that boy on the beach. The sun crosses overhead, beyond midday, and burns in the background. The breeze carries their deepening voices—their laughter, their rallying cries—out to sea. The water is lowering, emptying the marsh, leaving behind mud that is wet and thick and perfect for throwing. They hurl wads of earth at each other across grassy inlets. They jump and climb and hide, squealing in a way that's only allowed here. They are lost in their play, their childhood extended another day. As the sky turns from clear blue to rich orange, lips begin to shiver on the toddlers along the shore, so parents wave them in. Adults don't go out after them. The grass is too sharp, the mud gets deep and eats shoes, the water could freeze you after a while. It is only theirs. They resist. They rinse. With nods and waves, they part. Reality suspended for the day, just mere hours of enchantment, leaves them deeply satisfied, connected. They don't speak of it. On a slow walk back, they transition and return to the world. They don't know it yet, but this sacred space that lets grown boys play is the story of their lives.

The Trailblazing Generation

I believe that current twentysomethings were the first generation truly raised online. They were using AOL Instant Messenger and cell phones as tweens in middle school, and navigating MySpace and Facebook long before the rest of us. To me, they are the portable-technology trailblazing generation. They were raised on social technology almost all of their lives. It was part of their way. And many parents during those years were behind the learning curve. Kids and teens would use the technology, create accounts, change passwords, and stay one step ahead of parents. Parents caught on by reading newspaper articles or talking about concerns with other parents. Once they set limits, the technology would change again. It has happened so fast, especially for children coming of age since the turn of the millennium. It went from dial-up and desktops to pocket-sized, lightning-fast communication in a blink. They were our global guinea pigs. We saw the impact of technology, the pros and cons, the obsession and challenges, through their experiences. And it shocks me now to hear how surprised young adults in this age group are by the overuse of technology by such young children now. One young woman said to me, "Seeing eleven-year-olds with iPhones freaks me out!" So I decided to reach out and ask those twentysomething trailblazers what advice or thoughts they would give a tween or teen today about technology. It included:

○ Use it for communication; the world has become a scarier place and it is good to have something near so you can be safe, but, that being said, don't let it ruin your growth.

○ Don't confuse phone communication with face-to-face communication.

○ I think it is hard for a young teen to understand this right now, but looking back, I am glad my parents kicked me off the computer and told me to go outside.

○ Don't say something over text or online that you wouldn't say to someone's face. I've learned that the hard way.

○ Social networking is so distorted because everyone posts the good things and "look how great my life is," and it can affect young kids who compare themselves to others when it's not real.

○ Don't sneak it or try to look at it in class or at work or when people are talking to you. It's rude and everybody knows what you're doing. Ask to be excused for a minute if you need to text or call someone.

○ Time flies when you're surfing Twitter or the Internet when you could be getting homework done instead. Social media makes it SO easy to procrastinate on homework; same with texting—it also can be incredibly distracting.

○ Stop taking selfies, be a high schooler and live in the moment because those years of your life are some of the best.

○ No one really cares about your daily schedule—if you went to school or the gym or whatever. Post stuff with meaning and don't forget you can't take back what you tweet or post.

○ Get outside, hang with friends, and participate in activities that I'm sure can provide more satisfaction than any cell phone.

I think their overall message can be summarized as that phones should not replace real, personal communication and real experiences. In fact, they're preaching exactly the essence of this chapter: Be present. Since the explosion of the use of smartphones and laptops, it's not just young people who are plugged in now. I think more than anything, we are all hoping to preserve authenticity—be our real selves, talk in person, say what we mean, pay attention to the places and people around us.

This exercise also shows the power of reflection. Many of the young adults that contributed said it felt "therapeutic" to analyze their tech use and advise a younger person. I think we all could benefit from bringing our self-awareness to life by asking ourselves questions about our beliefs and motivations. The better we know ourselves, the better we parent!

FOMO: Fear of Missing Out

Recently I was chatting about the details of this book with a family friend and college sophomore, Matt. He said that his one message to his generation or young people using technology would be to live your own life. He thinks it's easy to become envious or feel bad for yourself when it looks like everyone else is constantly posting about their awesome, amazing good times. He believes that most people share online only to make *everything* look awesome and amazing. And it's just not. Kids and teens are doing boring, lame things without their friends all the time. They just market their lives as super fun. And soon everyone is outdoing each other with the staged fun times and it's easy to be caught in that trap. It feels like everything needs to be the time of your life. And most kids don't even realize it's happening. They feel bad or left out or bored after one look through their news feed and they can't pinpoint what triggered that feeling.

I think this is a great perspective because it has happened to me too. I'll be having a fine day, contented with whatever is happening, and suddenly, after a scroll through Facebook, I'll think, *Should we be apple picking today too?* or *Should we be out enjoying the last beach day of the season?* Though I'm not always aware of it, my fun anxiety really kicks up. *Eek! What if my family isn't having enough fun? What if my kids are missing out? What if we sit around and do nothing today? If we just lie on the couch or clean out closets—it will be a total parenting fail! What will the kids share as their weekend news on Monday?* And that's a slippery slope, because it will never feel like enough. We always feel like we should be doing more.

I also want my children to have the freedom to be themselves without always posting or sharing where they are, what they're doing, and who they are with.

Online Personalities

And what about online personalities? Have you ever had a conversation with your child about the person they portray themselves as online? Perhaps they are more confrontational, flirtatious, sexual, confident, or honest online than they are in person. Maybe they don't say much at all. This is a big source of conversation in our house. We are constantly discussing teens' behavior and how kids choose to present themselves online. We have discussed how some girls are eager to text or share, comment, like, and respond to something online, but would never be comfortable having a conversation in person at school. Or how a kid who is unsure of himself at school is acting like a wiseass or a tough guy online. It is easier to be brave when the communication isn't face-to-face. Perhaps who they are in school isn't really them and the online personality is more authentic.

We cannot control the behaviors of others. We can't judge choices another person makes online. We can only encourage our children to think for themselves. We can discuss, learn from, and crystalize our own values and philosophies based on the actions of others. Ask questions.

○ Have you ever seen someone act completely different online than they do at school?
○ Do you think it's easier to be honest or more real online?
○ Why do you think she shared that picture of herself?
○ Who is he talking to like that? Is he usually that aggressive at school? Why do you think he does it online?
○ Have you tried talking to her in class? Maybe if you start a conversation first, it will flow like it does online.

You can talk about the choices that peers make or observe and digest certain behaviors. But you can also talk about your child's choices. Doing this gives us a better understanding of what they hope to gain from social networking. What message are they sending about themselves? Is who they are online who you see in person? Do they say and do things in generally the same way online—humorously, seriously, sarcastically, shyly—as they do in person? Do you know the child that is presented online—can you recognize them? Take notice. Again, ask questions. Not in a drill-and-kill firing of questions, but as a natural part of the dialogue. Here are some examples:

○ Can I see your profile pic? Why did you choose that one?
○ Is it fun to post and talk about the Celtics in real time with your friends? You guys love stats!
○ Tell me about that video that you shared. Where did you find it?

○ I noticed you haven't really been posting anything lately. Is everything okay? Are you taking a break from Twitter?

○ Have you ever had a public disagreement online? How did you handle it?

Girl Love, #Hashtags, and Other Online Behaviors

Here is a trend I have noticed. Have you seen it? A teen girl posts a picture of herself, maybe showing off her hair, nail polish design, or a new outfit. It's a pretty standard photo. But then eighty girls immediately like the picture and comment, "You're perfect," "hot," "amazing," "jealous," "gorgeous," "best hair ever," "love those shorts." What is all of this gushing? What if you don't love or like a picture? What are the social consequences? What if no one drools over the very same, very typical picture that your child posts? How does that feel? As parents, these are the pieces of social networking we need to look more closely at. These are the places where insecurity or anxiety might blossom.

The online culture for girls can be overwhelming. The pressure to post and respond is heavy. I see appearance being a primary focus of the posts and shares of teen girls and young women—hair, clothes, accessories, shoes, nails, makeup, eyeballs. The substance and thoughtfulness on display can be quite limited. As are the responses. I see the identity of a high school sophomore shrink to her hair worn wavy one day and flat ironed the next. I know there is more (so much more!) to her story. We must encourage our girls to post ideas, thoughts, creative work, and accomplishments, to contribute in a more meaningful way. Tags like "popular" or "pretty" might corner a girl into resisting posting about herself beyond the physical. If one girl gets ninety likes for a selfie and another girl gets eight, how does that feel? What happens to self-esteem and self-confidence when worth is reduced to "likes"? Ask your daughter about this! Look at her accounts and shares; what is happening for her online?

I gathered several young women (working professionals in their early twenties) and asked them what subjects and topics females post about and share online. They all agreed that most of their friends and co-workers post about shoes, fitness, and pretty drinks and share endless selfies. One of the women responded, "It gets tricky for me. I like posting articles or starting conversations online about my opinion, yet I feel insecure posting my interests at times . . . because it's not always accepted by social media audiences. I don't want to seem preachy or out of context."

I can see this reflected online, as well. So, if this is how a college graduate feels, a tween or young teen must feel like it's impossible to be her true, whole self online. Consider this when teaching your daughter. Consider the pressure, the expectations, and the social consequences of sharing online. Male or female, even as adults, we all want to be liked and accepted. Be a guide for your children as they grow and develop themselves online for their entire social world to see. Encourage them to take a risk and show who they really are. Long-eyelash close-up shots can be fun and can have their place, but what excites your daughter? What does she love? Help her practice sharing a little (or a whole lot!) of that.

Recently I interviewed a family that does not allow social networking accounts for their high school–age daughters. They have smartphones and are able to text, but both parents agree that delaying joining the social networking sites like Instagram and Twitter is best for their girls. When I asked the mother about her decision, she said, "I just see and hear about so much trouble for the girls online. I don't feel like I'm punishing Katie, I feel like I'm preventing her from having the headaches. The texting and picture sharing are enough for them." This is a unique perspective, especially for parents of teens. I don't hear a lot of families saying no. She continued, "I feel like they're documenting everything. Last night we hosted a sleepover, and Katie's friend tweeted over and over again about her every move. Seriously? Aren't they boring themselves sharing all of these everyday details?"

I asked Katie what she thinks about all of this. Does she feel left out or is she mad at her parents about these limits? She said she understands what they are doing. She and her parents talk about everything, so they know about a lot of what goes on online from the stories she shares with them about her friends and classmates. Katie said she feels really close to her parents and trusts that their rules are designed to protect and help her, not because they don't trust her. Sometimes at school, she told me, someone will reference a picture or post from Instagram and she'll say, "I don't know what you're talking about. Remember? I don't have Instagram!" Katie doesn't feel like she's missing out on too much, because her friends text her all the time too. Someday she wants to have social networking accounts, she said, but for now, she doesn't need them. She doesn't need another thing to worry about. She agrees with her parents that not being on social networking has saved her both time and headaches.

 Try This!

E-tox Yourself! Start with a one-day or a whole-weekend e-tox! This is a chance for everyone in the family to detox from electronics. This isn't a form of punishment, and the time should be filled with deliberate distractions, adventures, and device-free family fun! When your e-tox is over, take some time to talk about what was hard or easy, how being disconnected made everyone feel, and how you used the time when you would have been plugged in. Can your family make it a regular occurrence? Go for it!

Katie's response was similar to what I hear from teen girls all the time. They love their phones. But they are often so relieved when their phone is lost, damaged, or taken away by their parents. Yes, that is correct. Our children feel relief when they don't have their phones. That is how much energy it requires of them. Without them, they don't need to manage them—all the worrying, checking in, responding, obsessing, and connecting simply vanish. And they can let go. Recently I have heard that adults are deliberately going on "digital diets" or "e-toxing" because their addiction has become so intense. Perhaps this is a practice we can incorporate into our lives together with our children.

I give this example to families all of the time: If your children were eating rows and rows of cookies at a time, every day, they would get sick. Hopefully you would intervene, tell them to put the cookies away. Perhaps you would take a break from buying cookies for a few weeks. Think of parenting the technology in the same way. Do not let them gorge on technology, do not allow them to become sick or addicted from overusing it. A mother shared with me that when her daughter's phone was taken away as a consequence of something she did, her girl was literally shaking and trembling from the anxiety it caused. She was showing real signs of addiction and withdrawal. It was a major eye-opener for the family, showing them how great the *need* to have the phone had become for their daughter. What would happen to your child if the technology suddenly vanished? Would it be hard for them to let go? Would they melt down? Or would they carry on? How tightly connected is your child to technology and how can you make sure there is tech-free space in every day? Incorporate these ideas and thoughts into your iRules. If your child shows signs of being a chronic tech user, set regular times for that child to be without it before it becomes a problem. Set strict boundaries. Make it nonnegotiable and encourage your child to fill that time with something important or meaningful to them. If that is not enough and you feel like your child or teen is truly suffering from tech or online addiction, please speak to your pediatrician. Living in the modern world and completely abstaining is probably not realistic. Create strategies that meet the needs of your child, even if you need the assistance of professionals.

I spoke to a group of teens and asked for their insights on what the rules are for boys and girls posting to social networking sites. At first they were hesitant, not sure what I meant by "rules." So I prompted them with questions: "Can boys post selfies?" I was answered with a resounding "NO! Well, only funny ones, not serious." "What do girls usually post about?" and "Have you ever wanted to post something online but didn't because it wasn't 'cool'?" A discussion is sparked by my asking if social networking accounts and posts reflect who people really are. Or is it safer to just post what everyone posts about? I ask Greg some of these questions too. He gives me this feedback: "I love the Beatles. But I wouldn't post a screenshot of the *Yellow Submarine* album because it would go unseen, meaning no one would care because no one [but me] really listens to that stuff. It doesn't matter online, so I wouldn't post about it. Even though it's a really big part of what I love, I know it wouldn't interest anyone. It's not relevant." A few of the boys I talk to think that girls have more freedom to post a variety of stuff online, but they all agree that no one—boys or girls—really posts anything of substance. They tell me there's just stuff you post about yourself and stuff you don't. It's not that they're guarding who they are, they tell me; they know they are brighter and have more to say than what they post online, but it's just not socially acceptable. Together, we draw up the list below.

The Rules according to Teens

> **Girls Can Post:** selfies, outfits, mirror pics, pets, nails, face shots, quotes, pics with friends, birthday collages, anything brand name, bedroom décor, beach or vacation scenes, sports, popular music that everyone likes

Girls Can't Post: "too-much-skin selfies," rude remarks, too-much-makeup or done-up selfies, inappropriate pictures of themselves with drugs or alcohol, too many pictures of family, anything that copies someone else

Boys Can Post: anything sports related, uniforms, sneakers, socks, stylish clothes, paychecks, pictures from the classroom, pics with friends, food, popular music screenshots like Eminem or Jay Z, playing an instrument to cool music

Boys Can't Post: selfies, anything—songs, quotes, images, styles, language—perceived as "girlie"

If nothing else, we can see that there is social pressure to be accepted and behave in accord with a certain set of mores created by our peer culture. Even though they insist that if someone did violate a peer rule, they wouldn't care. One of the girls chimes in, "People have a right to do whatever they want on their own accounts." The boys say they might tease a buddy if he shared a poem or something corny, but it would just be in fun. As parents we can tune in to the online social culture and ask our children some of these very questions. Are they able to fully express themselves online? Or are they playing it safe? How can we encourage our kids to let all they have to offer shine out online? Encourage your kids, both boys and girls, to take a risk online by sharing a thought, song, article, idea, or something that makes them stand out as the authentic individual that they are.

Then there are hashtags. Hashtags, hashtags everywhere. Some pictures are loaded with a dozen or more hashtags. Hashtags have a number sign (#) preceding them. You might remember it as the pound sign. Now it signifies something that's "trending," meaning a popular topic regarding current events, sports, entertainment, food, and more. A typical tweet with a hashtag would look like this (stolen directly from Greg's Twitter): "Doubleheader on Martha's Vineyard #baseball

#ferrycrew #summerball." If I click on any of the words with a "#" attached, they will bring up posts and pictures of everyone (followers or not) that has used a hashtag for, say, "baseball." It also allows the person posting to be part of something larger and gives a sense of belonging while also allowing users to gain followers.

Let's talk about the power of followers. When a user's number of followers increases, there is a sense of approval and acceptance from the online community. It translates into feelings we all can relate to: *I want to belong. I want to feel popular. I want to be seen.* An increased number of followers usually results in increased numbers of likes, comments, and shares. This can make a tween or teen (or a full-grown adult) feel validated and important. *I matter in the world!* That can be a powerful feeling. This is a subject ripe for conversation in a home with teens.

Try This Conversation Starter: *"How many friends or followers do you have?" "Do you know them personally?" "Do you talk to them at school or during activities?" "Does it feel more important to have a lot of followers, or followers that you personally know and like?" See where this takes you. It will be a nice opportunity to assess your child's online personality and preferences.*

Meet Kellie

My sister Kellie is a twenty-five-year-old professional recruiter in the technology field. She lives and works in Boston. She has degrees in communication studies and education with a focus on gender studies and media. In addition to that, she is much hipper and cooler than I am. I asked her to help me cut through the fog of followers and hashtags in young, modern culture and give it to me straight.

I asked her this question: "What's the benefit to having more followers if you aren't a famous person or someone with a product to sell?"

The Kellie Report: I would say street cred, proof of popularity, a tangible showcasing of how your images are favorable for a certain audience, earned respect or appreciation from particular social realms: indie, hipster, artsy, fashion, health, fitness. Also, followers are used for a display of legitimacy. The more followers you have the more "legit" you are. On the other hand, if you have an account without any pictures uploaded, have minimal followers, but are following many people—you are a creeper. Reason being, you aren't contributing to Instagram and are most likely scrolling through pictures that came from specific hashtags you've searched. I've heard about guys who have created an Instagram account just to look at pictures of women that they may know or don't know—famous and not famous. As you can imagine, I don't accept follower requests from these types of people.

There are zillions of trends to join, and some are hardly trends at all, but they send a message or get a point across. Hashtags can name your location, who's in the picture with you, a memory, or an idea. I see a picture of a friend on vacation and the hashtags read #beachbums, #caribbean, #equator, #nokids, #frozendrinks, #sunburn, #getaway, #besthubbie, #anniversary, #nevercomingback, and so on. These hashtags support the picture and perhaps communicate what the person posting really wants to say. It becomes clear what is happening on her trip, what she is doing, who she is with, why she is there in just a few words. Sometimes a hashtag can protect us from being judged.

The Kellie Report: If I'm posing for a picture with a group of my single girlfriends during a night out and put #single upon uploading it, the message I'm trying to convey could be anything from "single and happy" or "proudly single" to "ask me out!" However, if we are making goofy faces, are in pj's, or are eating mass amounts of food and upload the picture with a

#single, the message changes. It then becomes more of a sarcastic, wiseass connotation, as if stating, "single and here's why!" Another common example is if I upload a picture of a giant ice cream sundae or a huge steak dinner, I'd use hashtags that will say things like #pigout or #chowing to protect myself from being judged. That message is more like "I'll say what you're thinking!"

I often look at hashtags as representing what the user is *really* trying to say—the story behind the post or the story behind the photo. Even I do it! Once I posted about Greg's concussion that I insisted was a head cold. Then I wrote #motheroftheyear, #oops. The message is—I made a mistake and feel like an idiot. But I use a sarcastic hashtag to help make light of it and share my mistakes with other parents. One scroll through my pictures reveals friends' and followers' hashtags that read, #nomakeup, #relaxed, #selflove, #lovemydog, #nightout, #memories, #wishmeluck, #allyoucaneat, #fullmoon, #love, #sadface, #wifelife, #capecod. You can imagine a photo or a story to accompany each of these hashtags. So when you view your child's accounts or see their posts, check out the hashtags; you might get more of the story. You might even get the whole story! Or at least the very message they are trying to convey.

Keep a lookout for common (and ever-changing) online personal games and quizzes. They can be harmless—and mostly are—but sometimes behind the scenes, there can be more to the story. An example of these types of games is "Truth is . . . ?" If you post this on Instagram and someone likes that post, then you would post a true (to you) comment about that person. I will give you some examples (sans user names) from a day when Greg played this game on Instagram in seventh grade. Below are his responses to the people that liked his post, which means they wanted to hear Greg's version of the truth about them. And they wanted to see it and read it publicly.

GH: Truth is you are the man. You are awesome.

GH: Truth is I haven't talked to you in a while. You are wicked nice.

GH: Truth is you are a quiet girl and we need to talk more.

GH: Truth is you are hilarious.

GH: Truth is you are one of the coolest girls I have ever met. You are so real and true to yourself. Let's be better friends.

GH: Truth is you seem cool.

GH: Truth is you're on my team. You are the man and my hoops bro.

It carries on like this for hundreds of comments. I am obviously delighted that his responses are basically harmless. Sometimes in the multiple responses he gives on his profile online, I can tell when he's being polite and when he genuinely likes someone based on the memories and inside jokes he shares or the specificity of his answer. When you were twelve or thirteen, wouldn't it have been awesome to hear how people *truly* felt about you? How can this not be enticing and addicting? But I think it's probably clear where this game can sometimes lead. Even a simple comment like "I don't know you" can feel harsh to a person eager to hear a positive response. I also notice how often girls label each other "best friends." How does it feel if you don't get this label or are excluded? How do our children process that? Some comments can be misinterpreted, mean-spirited, or just plain awkward. Not to mention that all comments are public. So if a peer decides to say something negative, cruel, or embarrassing, it is visible to all.

To take it even a step further, there are apps and Web sites that allow anonymous questions to be asked and answered, like QuizYour Friends.com, a program that kids use on social networking sites to create a personal quiz for their peers to complete. It's popular because it's supposed to answer the question "How well do you know me?" Most of the quizzes are innocent, with multiple-choice questions like "Who is my favorite athlete?" But we always want to look for the silent message, for what goes unsaid and the impact that has. For example, think about questions like "Who is the prettiest girl in our grade?" or "Who is my best friend?" How does it feel if you aren't listed as the correct answer or are excluded as a choice altogether? There is also Ask.fm, a new social networking site that's quite popular with teens and tweens right now. Users post questions anonymously. A question I like to ask my children when they are experimenting with something new online is this: "Does this game [site, app, activity] make your life better?" After some discussion about Ask.fm, Gregory decided to delete his account. It wasn't adding anything positive to his life.

Sites and quizzes like these can seem harmless but lead to silent aggression ("silent" because there is no obvious accountability) in emotional relationships that can damage self-esteem and self-worth. Another trend includes "like for a grade," where, for example, you grade the person who likes the post by designating a category:

A+: I couldn't live without you.
A: Best friends
B+: We're close
B: Friends
C+: We've talked before . . .
C: I like your account
D+: I don't know you
F: I don't like you . . .

When you look around and see the collection of ways our children can be put down, it's exhausting. I hope I have brought some of the ways our kids use media to communicate and express themselves to your attention. It is understandably overwhelming. Seeing all that is happening for our children online can bury a parent. I am pretty sure I've just scratched the surface here, so my advice to you is this: Pay attention. If it isn't clear right now why our children need to step away from phones and computers and social networking accounts on a regular basis, I'm not sure what I could say to convince you. It can suck them in and become central to their existence. Please set some boundaries and create iRules for your children and teens so they don't go insane grading each other or publicly rating their peers.

If you take nothing else from this book, know this for sure: Nothing matters to your child like your love, acceptance, and guidance. There is no rating game, anonymous quiz game, or number of Instagram followers that will replace your presence in their lives. They may have their feelings hurt sometimes. They may even have their feelings hurt a lot of times. We will feel a very strong urge to prevent that from happening. Sometimes we will. Other times we will not. We cannot put out all of the fires, nor should we. We need to raise resilient children. Our children can (and will) feel hurt, sad, and confused during their lives. We need to teach them to process those feelings and rise again. They need to know that at their core, they are whole, valued, important people and that no online opinion will ever change that.

iRule Tip: Let your child be the teacher. Ask questions! Do you want a lesson on Twitter or hashtags? Do you see something online (like a quiz game) and not understand it or how it impacts your child? Ask! Our kids are more eager than you think to teach us about their online world. They are a wealth of information. When we ask questions, we usually get a larger conversation in return.

7

Technology Is Fun

iRule: Embrace and Enjoy

> **My iRule:** Download music that is new or classic or different from what millions of your peers are listening to. Your generation has access to music like never before in history. Take advantage of that gift. Expand your horizons.

> **My iRule:** Play a game with words or puzzles or brainteasers every now and then.

The gifts of technology are plenty. And I love those gifts! I love my iPhone, my GPS, my laptop, my iPad. I use the technology every day. I love the Facebook community. I have access to childhood, high school, college, and current friends all in one place. I feel connected to family members that live far away and cousins I've been out of touch with. This excites me! I love seeing the pictures of a classmate's new baby or hearing about an exciting new job opportunity for a community member. I use social networking professionally and personally. I love to FaceTime with family all over the country. I have built professional relationships with people all over the world because of technology. In fact, my very own iRules contract would never have been seen by the masses if it weren't able to spread like wildfire over the Internet. I reached out to my readers and asked them to identify what their favorite gifts of technology are. Here are some responses.

O *A friend is working overseas. But he can Skype with his baby on a daily basis. They are so lucky to have that technology to use.*

O *I'm an introvert who's lived in six different states. Technology helps me stay connected to friends and family who I otherwise would have completely lost touch with over the years. I travel a lot, and it's so amazing to meet up with old friends and be able to pick up where we left off. My son has also been able to build really strong friendships with a handful of kids who live far away or go to different schools—but he Skypes with them all the time. He has also had access to great learning opportunities through online classes in subjects he couldn't get locally.*

O *My dream job. I can only do it because I can work remotely via technology.*

O *I can only do my job with the use of technology. I program my GPS about six or seven times a day. If I had to rely on maps, I would be much less efficient and would probably not be in this practice area because map use is a definite weakness of mine. Also, we use tablets for all of our documentation. . . . Again, if it was all written by hand, this wouldn't be the job for me. As far as the kids go, they have had a lot more required computer use the last few years (including online games for reinforcement).*

O *It has allowed me to earn my degree. I took online courses while working full-time, raising a three-year-old, and pregnant. So certainly*

I would not have been able to finish otherwise. I also enjoy FaceTime with my sister who lives out of state. My daughter also has a friend that just moved to New Mexico and they are going to start [using] Skype/FaceTime too.

○   *I work for a hospital. You can be sitting in your doc's office complaining of a rash (for example), then the doc takes a picture and does an e-consult with the dermatologist. It's a win-win! Working in health care, I see the advantages of increased technology on a daily basis.*

I want families to see the value, the goodness in technology so they can explore and encourage its use by their children. Find a component of technology that you love, add guidelines for using it to your iRules, and celebrate it with your own family!

Music

I want to be sure that my children understand the power of the technology of their time. I want them to use it to its full potential for good, for their benefit. I think access to music is a perfect example of that.

Truth Alert: *If I wasn't married to Adam, then this iRule might not feel so important. He is a musician and music lover and has been for his entire life. Listening to music is active for him. And he shares that love with our children, so in our home this has become a priority, a vital piece of our lives.*

The ability to comb through all current and past music, whether successful or hidden, feels like a beautiful gift. I think it's exciting that all of us get to fully explore and listen to the music of our choosing. We can be selective or we can search, but I really want my kids to embody the spirit of seekers. Go looking for what truly interests them, not what is fed to them by the mainstream media. Of course they can love all of that stuff too if that's what they want. Mass media will always be there. But the idea that they can connect with just about any musician or artist in any genre fills my heart. It is important enough that music be celebrated in our home that it needed to be incorporated into our iRules.

And I see it work! I look through Greg's playlists and hear what is blasting from his room, and the varied range of interests thrills me. He'll listen to Eminem and Macklemore albums one day. And then another day, the Beatles' White Album or Pearl Jam. It's incredible. His playlist titled *Chill Out* has Mumford and Sons, Damien Rice, the Jackson 5, Weezer, Bob Marley. Talk about options!

Music opens dialogue for us about history, time and place, culture, image, media, language, art. Recently Greg was having a discussion with some peers about the lyrical content of some specific pop music.

 # A Music Note from Adam
The Positive Impact of Technology on Music and Families

- It allows you to listen to something without making an investment. You don't need to purchase an album or a single—you can stream it. Like it? Listen some more. Don't like it? Move on.
- It lets you explore genres. Having the ability to seamlessly transition from rap to rock to jazz to funk to musicals is important for musical development. How do you know what you like without exploring?
- Technology allows you to find new artists, and maybe discover that you don't like artists that you thought you did (because they were shoved down your throat by radio stations). It's an avenue to artist discovery. iHeartRadio. Pandora. Rdio. Spotify. They all offer artist radio stations

His buddies were preaching that it is of such good quality, but Greg was countering that it's fun, but impossible to connect to or feel the emotion of. Their response: "Okay, says the kid who listens to the Beatles." Greg still references this moment as one of the funniest (unintended) examples of understanding the power and story of music.

Because of Adam, my kids fall asleep listening to him play Paul Simon or Van Morrison on the piano. They listen to stories of growing up on everything from the Grateful Dead to Jim Croce to Pearl Jam to Ben Folds. It's part of our family story. It's important enough for him to bring the discussion, the music, the history into our home and marry it with the current technology so the access is deliberate, easy, and

that select similar artists for you. Rdio allows you to select how "brave" you want to be. I LOVE this feature.

I spent so much time listening to albums, reading liner notes, exploring music when I was a kid. I had to buy CDs, vinyl, etc. Bring it home, put it on the stereo, sit and listen. It was tactile—getting the story of the band or artist while listening to the music really helped me to get a feel for where the artist was coming from. It brought the music to life. Greg still does this—he wants the whole story. He wants it all to be a real experience.

That, to me, is the downside of technology: Consumption of music can be quick and thoughtless. No backstory. No investment. But overall, the power of technology allows for exploration, which I ultimately believe is positive for kids and the music industry. It just needs to be fostered a bit.

important. And Adam believes it to be equally important for the kids to connect with the music of their generation. The girls make up dance routines to Katy Perry and Taylor Swift songs all the time. Ella's eighth birthday party theme was a sing-along, and she made sure Adam knew and could perform all of her favorite music live. I watched this man rock out to Top 40 hits with about twenty-five little girls crammed around the piano singing along. He even took requests (thank you, iPad, for chord searches!).

But maybe this doesn't matter to you. Maybe music is not a priority for your iRules list. Perhaps there is something else that matters as much to you and your children as music does to us. Perhaps it can be brought into your home and nurtured using the technology. Talk about that! Bring that to life in a way that positively impacts your family. It's not about controlling the interests of our children; like everything, it's about balance. But being able to use the technology to introduce them and expand their exposure to aspects of life that matter to you is a treasured gift.

☑ **iRule Tip:** It takes a family! Because this contract is created from the perspective of family values and interests, it's important to reflect on the views of the entire family. Because my husband is a professional musician, the contract point about listening to all types of music was relevant because it applies to the interests and discussions of our family. Use your family's passions to take advantage of the technology!

iRule: Put Down the Controller

> **My iRule:** Play a game with words or puzzles or brainteasers every now and then.

Gaming

Smartphones are primary to our technology use. They appeal to all ages and include portable Internet access, social networking, a camera, games, apps, and texting. We work on them, we carry them with us on errands and outings, they are central to our lives. But what about everything else? What about all the other forms of technology besides smartphones? Where and how do your children play with their gaming technology? Perhaps they use devices like the Nintendo DS console, an iPad, an iPod, an e-reader, or video game systems like the ones my kids have. Perhaps they beg for and borrow your iPhone to play games on. Video games and apps have something for everyone and appeal to the masses. I asked my kids to list their favorite tech games and why they like them.

> **Gregory:** I love to play stealth and assassin games [an answer all mothers dream of hearing] on Xbox because of the graphics, plots, art, creativity, and excitement. I like games where I can be one of the characters. I feel [like] part of the game. I also love sports video games, because I just love being LeBron James and dominating everyone. Who wouldn't love that?
>
> **Brendan:** My favorite games are *Minecraft* and *Clash of Clans* because I can build my own world and also play with friends

both on the iPad and Xbox. I also like to play *Halo*—don't worry, Mom, there's no blood—because I get to play it only when it's just me and Daddy.

Ella: I like to play apps on the iPad. This weekend I played Subway Surfers and Food Fair. I get to use my imagination and make things. I like to find out about new apps.

Lily: I like the iPad apps like *Minecraft* and *Elo Milo*. I like building stuff and playing with Brendan and his friends. My favorite game on Xbox is *Fruit Ninja* because I get to do the chopping. I like when the games are different every time.

Cassidy: My favorite games on the iPad are *Hair Salon and Carnival Games*. I like to do their hair and make stuff myself. I learned the games from Brendan. Nan [my mother] also showed me these games she found while looking at apps for her students. [Her parting thought:] Mom, you seem like a different person when you ask me all of these questions for your book.

Because gaming comes in many forms today, we have had to make some iRules to manage them. We do not play video games or iPad or iPod apps or games during the school week. It was causing so many sibling battles, and I just couldn't make managing equal playing time a priority in our lives. This system runs smoothly and keeps game playing from being a central part of our lives, while still allowing access to it during weekends. This is similar to our television policy, though that's not as firm. The kids are usually out and about in the neighborhood until dinner, then doing homework and their hygiene routines, reading books, and going to bed. So if someone does watch television, they really need a break from it all—like when Cassidy wipes out on her bike and is banged up, Ella has a headache from the school bus—which is rare. The weather matters too. In the darkness of December, if they're clawing at each other and I'm checking things off my to-do list before day's end, *Electric Company* is my greatest friend.

Truth!

I hate video games—a lot. They don't move me, they don't interest me. I watch as Brendan, Gregory, and Adam flip for the graphics, the plots, the challenges, and I'm lost. I respect the art and genius of it—there are many times I am certain they're watching the weekend highlights on *SportsCenter*, but it's an Xbox game—and think it's amazing how evolved these games have become. But I don't want to play.

The Whole Truth!

When I was nine years old, I played *Super Mario Bros.* on Nintendo for so many hours and with such great intensity that my shin and calf muscles cramped up from constantly flexing and tightening them while trying to rescue the princess. It would make me cry, but it didn't stop me from playing. So I do get it. I just miss two-dimensional Mario and his innocence.

I'll admit there is this beautiful relief that exists here on Friday evenings when the kids come home after a full week of school and play. They curl up on the couch or with some friends to game away, watch a TV program of their choice, or enjoy app upon app. I'm not hustling them around, managing their homework and practice schedules, I just let them be. Fridays are usually a welcome gift, and the technology flows into the evening as a nice treat for them.

I believe our relationship with gaming to be in balance. I also find that some of these word and drawing games or apps can keep a family lighthearted and engaged; we can challenge each other when we're together or apart. It is silly to create a funny hairstyle or a huge ice cream sundae with toppings. We play *Draw Something* or *Sound Pop Quiz* or *Boggle* with a competitive spirit. Adam and our boys share a special connection through the culture of games—they read magazines about them, drool over systems and new releases, and visit game stores. They discuss the characters, much like we would after seeing a movie or reading a book. Sometimes it's important to use the technology for recreation and not take it so seriously.

I love nothing more than having a group of teenage boys piled in my house playing an Xbox sports game tournament (well, I love a lot of things more than that, but you know what I mean). They are having fun, enjoying each other's company, and being social. I hate nothing more than having a group of teenagers piled in my house playing games or chatting on their own devices, heads down, not engaged with each other, or playing a multiplayer game that is violent or unacceptable for younger siblings to see. There is a difference. If we revisit the idea of using technology with purpose, that difference becomes quite clear. How can we use technology to benefit and enhance our children's experiences, not dull them?

That being said, I recognize that it is grossly out of balance for so many. And I see how it can happen so easily. Video game addiction is an epidemic, especially for boys and teens. According to Education Database Online, 65 percent of US households play video games, and three out of five video game users are male. I've heard story after story of children of all ages, but especially boys, being locked into games, able to tune out the world for hours.

Tips for Parenting Gamers

- O Pay attention to video game ratings.
- O Preview games for content, language, and plot before buying them. Get educated.
- O Know the people with whom your children are gaming.

○ Think about young children and what they are seeing on the screens even if they are not playing. A game that is appropriate for a sixteen-year-old may not be okay for an eight-year-old to even view.

○ Preview games using gameplay trailers online before purchasing them.

○ Video game store employees are very eager to share their opinions and knowledge about specific games. On more than one occasion, we have had employees help us gauge the appropriateness of games for our boys.

○ Let gift givers like extended family members know your expectations or that you would like to approve video games for your children before they're given.

○ Talk to your children about games that interest them. Ask them why they like specific games. Tell them what you like and don't like about specific games. Create an ongoing dialogue and use examples.

○ Let it be social. Is your child an introvert? Parent-approved online gaming can help with socialization and making connections with peers. Is your child an extrovert? Hosting a group tournament can be a fun way to get kids together for some directed, engaged play.

○ Develop iRules establishing when play is acceptable. Having firm boundaries will eliminate struggles.

The Entertainment Software Rating Board (esrb.com) provides information to help parents and game users educate themselves on video games. Use its ratings system as a starting point for evaluating games, but be aware that you must still apply your family's beliefs and values to judge whether your children can purchase or play one. Become an educated consumer, and teach your child how to be a mindful consumer too.

Screens outside of Our Homes

A mother wrote to tell me that she attended a cross-country family reunion with her three-year-old daughter. She was so excited to introduce her daughter to so many cousins and other family members that she had never met. During that reunion weekend, the cousins, of all ages, spent their time primarily gaming. She was so disappointed that no adults had stepped in to limit the screen time. She was also frustrated because her daughter started begging, even throwing tantrums, to play the various devices as well. She couldn't peel her away. She explained that it was a tricky situation for her because she didn't want to offend her extended family, but she also felt like something

Try This!

Are you anticipating a big family gathering? I am a strong believer in being proactive instead of reactive with communication. Discussing things in advance can prevent a lot of sticky family situations. Try sending a group e-mail like this.

> Hi, everyone! I'm so excited to get all of the kids together for vacation next month. I know all of our kids are tech lovers, but I was hoping we could set aside some tech-free times during our trip. I think it's easier if we're all on board. Could we have one or two day trips without devices and maybe a few hours each morning as well? I'd hate for the kids to miss out on the family fun because they're plugged in the whole week. What do you think? I'd love to hear your thoughts on making this trip the best it can be for all of our families.

Truth: *It's important to note that I did test this on our extended family to see how they would feel about getting an e-mail like this. They thought it was both respectful and useful—especially if there had been an overuse problem or concerns in the past. It wasn't directed at one particular person or family and was casual in nature and sent in advance. They agreed that using a format like e-mail for communicating was easy for everyone to process and contribute to.*

---

precious was being lost to screen addiction in kids whose parents were not willing to parent the screens.

What about tech boundaries in other people's homes? Another mother was appalled that her young son's friend was allowed to play video games with what she thought were too-mature ratings. She was enraged when she found out that her own son had been playing them while visiting. She wrote to me asking for advice on how to confront the other parents and explain her boundaries. This calls for the most direct conversation possible, the less emotional the better: "Hi, Judy. I don't want Tommy playing that video game when he's at your house. It's not something he's allowed to play here, and I want to keep that consistent. Thanks for understanding." I believe family friends want to honor and respect other family friends. But they are not mind readers; they do not know what your standards are. Remember, every family has a different emotional temperature for technology. It is up to us, those leading our families, to advocate and speak up when necessary. Remember, be direct and keep it nonjudgmental for the most success.

This (true) text conversation with my friend Susan is a great example of how parents can communicate to make certain that tech behaviors are consistent with their families' varied needs. This convo is taken from an afternoon when my girls were playing with Susan's daughters at her house.

Susan: Hi, Janell, the girls are dancing, making up routines and video recording it. Now they want to post and share it on

YouTube. How do you feel about that? I don't really know anything about it.

Me: I'd rather they didn't post anything of themselves to YouTube.

Susan: Okay, I'm glad I asked. I wasn't sure. Thanks.

Me: Omg. This simple, direct conversation was awesome and prevented uncomfortable "after the fact" communication later on. I'm using this in my book as a bold example of parenting together. [Okay, I didn't say any of that, but I felt it.]

Parenting Tech in Two Places Tip!

It is best if all people actively involved in raising your children are part of the conversations about iRules (and all other rules). This can be especially important if your child is being parented in two households. It is best to have agreed-upon expectations that all parents and children created and understand. It is even better when the iRules are enforced equally too. I love this tip from a mother whose children are being raised in two homes where there is one set of iRules that everyone has agreed to follow. She says their motto is "It's not where the device is, it's whose hands it is in." That way her children understand that if they're at Mom's, Dad's, Nana's, or a friend's house, the same expectations apply. It's perfect!

It is also important to remember that maintaining consistent, deliberate communication between caregivers will make your iRules more effective. One of the questions I am asked most often about technology in two-home families is how to make it work. There is no realistic way for me to give a one-size-fits-all answer or a magical solution. Each family has its own unique story and circumstances. My parents divorced when I was an adult, but my sisters are much younger, so I saw the challenges that come with raising a family in two homes.

I have heard from so many families that, like the family described

iRules for Parents in Two Places (or Any Parents, Really!)

Resist the urge to parent via text! As challenging, emotionally intense, or annoying as it may be to have an in-person or phone conversation with the other parent in your child's life, please make the effort. Set some parenting iRules for each other as adults. Here are few imperatives that will help preserve healthy communication between parents.

○ No financial discussions are to take place via text messaging.

○ No health issues are to be discussed over text messaging.

○ No parenting concerns about the children—social, emotional, physical, personal—are to be discussed over text messaging.

○ No changes in plans are to be discussed over text messaging.

○ Establish weekly in-person or phone conferences to discuss any parenting or adult issues.

So what is safe for texting? Share a Google calendar, family pictures, unemotional information like "Leaving now to pick up the kids, be there in ten minutes," or "What is the address of the soccer field?" Make deliberate, mindful parenting a priority and create space to have dialogue with your child's other parent for the healthiest relationship.

above, have blanket iRules for both homes, but there are even more families that parent independently. This can be trickier, but parents need to find common ground to allow for some consistency. If your family situation is tense or your values vary, try to agree on one or two of the most important ground rules for both homes. The more our children have basic guidelines and rules that match between households, the more success both parents and households will have.

The Challenges

Just this weekend I experienced some resistance as I gathered my girls to do a jigsaw puzzle. They were cranky, Adam was out of town, and I was trying to have some family time without being plugged in or spending a fortune. The girls each eagerly contributed to the puzzle when I sat down, but if I got distracted and walked across the room or answered the phone, they would stop putting the pieces together and start nagging and teasing each other. It was frustrating. I wanted them to keep busy. But I realized that it might take me being fully present to get them committed to doing a project like a large puzzle. This awareness allowed me to sit still and fully engage until the project was complete. Everyone was more peaceful and proud when we all hung in there together. So sometimes, even when we pull out a board game or puzzle, it may take a little more work on our end to get it going. It might not be enough just to place it on the kitchen table and tell the kids to play. Eventually, as they get older, or when siblings lead them or it becomes a habit in your family, they may take to it quicker and drop into board game play with ease. But don't be discouraged if it doesn't "work" right away. And take their lead; they might just want Mom or Dad to stay undistracted and unplugged with them too.

Recently I have started to receive a lot of e-mails and questions from and have a lot of conversations with grandparents. They want to

A Plea to Remember the Board Games!

Tech play is convenient, fun, and sophisticated. But we must keep with the traditions of board games, jigsaw puzzles, card and dice games. Some of the warmest family memories and funniest jokes we have are from hysterical mishaps made during a game of charades or are of the ecstatic feeling (or enduring patience) of conquering a puzzle. These old games also foster learning, creative thinking, rule following, good sportsmanship, and turn taking. These connections build foundations for families and help to teach valuable life lessons.

A mother of three wrote to me saying that she wanted my readers to know that sometimes it is a challenge to get her kids into playing a game of Monopoly. But she doesn't give up! If she stays with it, if she is engaged and keeps encouraging them, the kids eventually relax and stop fussing. She is certain that everyone has way more fun over a board game together than over their keyboards in separate corners.

talk about the technology and the ways it is impacting their grandchildren. Their most common question is "How can I get my grandkids to stop using their computers [or phones or games] so much?" I start by asking them *why* their grandchildren are using them so often. Their response is usually—almost exclusively—"Their parents are so busy. And the kids are so busy, it's just easier to give them what they want when they're home. And they want their games." Then I ask them what they would do if they were the parents. How would it look? They tell me they would take the technology away, get rid of it completely, tell the kids to go outside, make it off-limits. But they often agree that it is "different now": The grandkids might be left out socially or left behind academically if they don't know how to use the technology with ease. It's the way of the modern world. They think it's hard to parent technology because using it is what the kids really want. It's more work to be a parent without it. One grandmother even admitted that when she watches her grandchildren, they behave much better if she lets them play their games. There's no fighting, she doesn't have to work to entertain them, and they're safe and happy. She says it's especially helpful on car rides—while she focuses on the road, the kids just keep to themselves and that makes it easier. So she totally understands why her son and daughter-in-law let the kids game so much, but it seems hard to enforce a boundary on use if the distraction is convenient for parents. But she goes on to say that they bring it everywhere, including to the dinner table, and she doesn't know when or where it stops.

I have a different perspective because each of my children does not have their own device. So my challenge lies in the sharing of technology. They cannot bring it everywhere with them, because there's not enough to go around. This is partly by design and partly just the circumstances of our family. The girls don't feel like they own a particular device, and therefore Adam and I still decide when and where use is appropriate. If they don't share, it goes away. And there are many Saturday mornings when, after a warning or two, the iPad is confiscated for wrestling or karate chopping and everyone must scrub a toilet or brush the dog to keep busy.

How to Parent the Gaming Challenges

O   Don't allow gaming to be central in your home. Keep a balance of activity, structure, and free time so that gaming is just one option out of many.

- Establish days and times for use as part of your family iRules.
- Identify acceptable games for each child in advance. Learn to play the games, read about them, listen to them, and trust the ratings.
- Designate nonnegotiable game-free times—during dinner, while doing homework, when outside and when friends are over, before school. Stick to them!
- Establish times when they are free to game, like a Friday afternoon or Saturday morning, when the kids can just dig in.

The Joys

Play doesn't have to be perfect! One day when Ella, Lily, and Brendan were really little, I was watching them run around our sectional couch chasing each other. They were being loud and wild while I was trying to quickly match up freshly laundered socks. For no reason, I just started throwing balls of matched socks at them and yelling "Sock bombs!" It was ridiculous fun, but five or six years later, they still remember this silly game we played one afternoon.

For years one of my favorite activities to do with Cassidy when she was in preschool and all of her older siblings were at school was to take her to the coffee shop and play the card game Uno with her. I absolutely loved and cherished this time with her. Here are a few reasons why I think those moments were so precious:

- I was away from my house, work, and responsibilities.
- I was having my coffee. She was having a muffin. How could we *not* be happy?
- It didn't cost a lot of money.
- It was often spontaneous.
- It didn't take forever. We'd spend just thirty minutes sitting together before moving on.

○ She had my full attention, so it felt special.

○ It was age appropriate. When she was very little, we would modify the game so the cards were laid out in front of her on the table. When she got older, she felt proud that she could hold them all in her hand so I couldn't see.

During a recent blizzard, most of our region lost power for an extended period of time. After it was over, I had so many families writing to me saying it was the best thing that had happened to them in years! Homes were without power and a state mandate to stay off the road was enforced, so the families in our community had to get creative. They played cards and board games, napped, and swapped stories by candlelight. They shoveled, built snowmen, and went sledding together. I heard numerous feel-good stories about neighbors sharing firewood and food and helping to care for each other's children. In our own home, we had to use our camping gear to make our morning coffee on the grill outside. I don't think my kids will ever forget the joy on my face when my husband brought me that cup of coffee!

My in-laws are the masters of preserving the spirit of childhood. Recently Adam took the kids over for an afternoon while I worked. They played board games, walked nature trails, read stories, baked cookies, and even played a sunset game of hide-and-seek. When they were asked at school on Monday to share their "weekend news," my children said the highlight of their weekend was "when Pups climbed a tree to hide from us but left a trail of cracker crumbs so we knew right where he was." They told me this story over and over—each of them in their own age-appropriate words. Their eyes were shining, and they giggled and smiled as they recalled these special moments. These few hours, doing simple things with people who cherish them, made their lives better. I believe this. I live by this.

Do these stories and examples mean that I'm nostalgic? Is it my attempt to remember the good old days? In a way, play is my connection to my past, my childhood. But it is also a gift. I don't see honoring experiences that are now atypical in our fast-paced culture as senti-mental, I see it as meaningful. Referring to the Slow Tech movement, a parent asked me, "What's the point? Why slow down when there is so much available to us?" I loved this question! The only response I could manage was simply "These pieces of life—they ARE THE POINT!" Okay, I didn't yell. It was more excitement than anger. True value is added to our lives when we connect with the people in our homes, in our fami-lies, in our neighborhoods and communities.

I encourage you to ask yourself what is meaningful to you. Since my children were babies, I have believed that reading to the kids, being outside with the kids, and watching them be present during imagina-tive play are the most sacred and special moments of our lives together. It unlocks a feeling within me that I can only describe as ancient, as bliss. What are the parenting moments when you feel this way? How can you cultivate them in your family life? What makes you shout "THIS IS THE POINT!" from the rooftops? Figure out what those things are for you and then do them—not because you are longing for the past or are afraid of the modern world—do them because they are the most important pieces of life to you.

iRule Tip: Video, computer, app, and portable games and systems are here to stay, so we must coexist! Take inventory in your house: If the kids weren't gaming, what would they be doing? What are children missing out on when they're gaming? Here's a sample of what my kids are not doing or getting when they're gaming.

○ Fresh air

○ Exercise

○ Creative play (most online games have set plots and purposes)

○ Being imaginative

○ Face-to-face interaction with peers

○ Exploring

○ Starting a conversation

○ Reading a book

Eyes Up and Heart Open

iRule: Live and Love

> **My iRule:** Keep your eyes up. See the world happening around you. Stare out a window. Listen to the birds. Take a walk. Talk to a stranger. Wonder without googling.

These final points truly reflect my iRules contract's core message. These points are a prayer, a meditation, a wish, a blessing for not just my own family and myself, but the world. I hope that we always maintain our human connection, our oneness, our curiosity. According to a 2011 report on a survey done by AVG Technologies, more young children can open a Web browser, use a smartphone, or play a computer game than can ride a bike, tie their shoes, or swim unaided. These changes in our children are very real. But we can be the people that foster a place where classic forms of play and pretend, checkers and coloring, coexist with the fastest and most exciting technology. It is up to us.

I talked with Lenore Skenazy, author of *Free-Range Kids,* who said that there are many ways in which the widespread use of technology can impact our children and their ability to develop and rely on themselves. According to Skenazy, parents in this culture are often led to believe that "no child is ever safe unless they are constantly supervised literally or electronically." This is changing childhood. When our children are out of our view, can they make decisions for themselves? Are our children able to take responsibility for their actions? Can they assess if a tree branch is safe to climb or if they are actually hungry for another cookie without asking us or when we are not physically present to give our approval?

During our discussion, I was reminded of a time when Greg went to the movies with his friends when he was about eleven years old. When he arrived, the movie was sold out. He called from a friend's cell phone and said, "What should I do?" My response was "I trust you to figure that out." He didn't like my answer, but I really wanted him to problem solve. A few hours later, when he returned home, I asked what he ended up doing. He said, "The other movies showing weren't appropriate, so we went to the arcade instead." I thought this was a great decision and was encouraged by the idea that he didn't really need my input, he used his own good judgment. Preserving these developmental skills and not allowing the technology to become, as Skenazy puts it, "an umbilical cord that doesn't get cut" serves their best interests.

Often devices are purchased with the assumption that we can then "breathe easy" as parents, when in fact the ability to constantly connect with our children leaves us nervous and often in panic mode when we are not able to reach them. The technology is marketed to us to be used as a constant, immediate necessity. Skenazy does believe that technology can be a healthy part of children's lives without fearing

Hey Parents, Keep Your Eyes Up Too!

○ Don't let work follow you home and invade every corner of your family time.

○ Designate times when you put your phone away. Don't get lost in the phone zone, constantly telling your kids to "wait" and "hold on" while you do something more pressing online.

○ Set boundaries. Practice telling people, "Tomorrow is a better time for me to talk," or "I have five minutes." Then stick to it.

○ Leave your phone behind and go!

○ Do something to benefit yourself and your family, not for the benefit of how it appears on your social networking account.

○ Be a curious being. Think about it. Talk about it. Let it sit. Try not knowing the answer.

○ Be fully present in your body. Use your senses. Try moving, speaking, or breathing just a little slower than you normally do. Notice.

○ Stay still when your children are talking to you—even if it's just once a day. Really hear them when they speak; look into their eyes, give a thoughtful response.

that letting them game, interact, or play will ruin them. Technology does not need to be another thing parents feel afraid of or guilty about. Rather, it is part of the changing times.

How This Book Made Me Better

I am so guilty. I find myself constantly telling my children to "wait" and "hold on" while I scroll through my phone for personal or professional e-mails. A response feels crucial, this e-mail needs my focused attention, this video is poignant, this article is hysterical. I can't stop looking at my phone. As I began creating Greg's iRules and speaking to parents, families, teens, and communities about technology, it became clear that I needed to walk the walk. I had to start integrating Slow Tech Parenting methods into my own life. It occurred to me that I have never heard a parent in any of the conversations or workshops say that they wish their child had more time to play video games or text. Most parents and families are craving a deeper connection. I knew I needed to make changes, and that even small changes could make a huge difference in my parenting life and beyond.

With these small changes in habits and awareness, my parenting has really improved. I realized that we do not need to have perfect behaviors as parents. We are flawed. We are dealing with the influx of technology just like our kids. But we can be aware of our actions to become stronger, more effective models for our children. The technology is new for all of us, we must come together to carve out and honor the importance of our deepest connections. Begin to carve out space for your behaviors to shift. It is work! It is easier to pass them your phone to play games on while they wait or to plug in the DVD in the minivan, but we owe it to our children to start somewhere, to make one small change away from being distracted and plugged in each day to embrace the slow times and be more connected as a family. We do not need to eliminate the technology; we just don't need to be ruled by it.

The Changes I Made

Change: No social networking sites, e-mail, or social chatty texts from 4:00 p.m. (when the kids arrive home from school) through bedtime. This is hard and not always consistent, but it is the goal.

Result: I interact with the kids more. I'm less snippy. I'm a better homework helper. I don't rush through making dinner and I seem to enjoy the process more. I might even do a load of laundry or sweep the floor at this time, giving the return of the entire family at night a more simplified feel.

Change: Wacky Wednesday! Every Wednesday the boys walk to Adam's office from school and they have some time together. I pick up the girls at the end of their school day and we have a little date. We keep it simple, in town, and on the cheap—an ice cream, a trip to the town library, a hike. We are usually home by 6:00 p.m., when we all gather back together for dinner. The catch—I leave my phone home or locked in the car!

Result: I am away from the house, work, and technology and get to spend deliberate time with my girls doing something together. I am present and engaged. It's a really positive midweek connection that everyone looks forward to.

Change: I notice the impact of my use of technology on those around me.

Result: I try very hard not to let my tech behaviors affect other people—in public, at home, while driving, in conversation, in parenting.

Talk to a Stranger

I received some criticism for encouraging Gregory to "talk to a stranger" in his original iRules contract. To me, "stranger" is not a synonym for murderer or pedophile, it means someone new. I certainly educate my children on trusting themselves, controlling and preventing what they can, knowing their surroundings, relying on the kindness of others, and using safety smarts when out and about in the world. However, striking up a conversation with a new kid at school, the guy at the sub shop, or someone at the park is healthy and normal behavior. Teaching my children that everyone has something to offer and something to teach is an important aspect of my personal philosophy.

One of my favorite times of the day is when I take morning walks with my girls. Each morning before school, one of the girls joins me on a one-mile walk around the neighborhood. Just today, Lily and I were on our morning walk with the dogs and we bumped into a man I recognized from our neighborhood walking his dog. He's an older man, he walks his little dog quite a bit, but I had never talked to him before. Today, Lily and I stopped and chatted with him for about ten minutes or so. He told us that his dog was sick from eating acorns at doggie daycare and the vet bills were steadily increasing. He asked us about our dogs—is our big white one hard to walk on the leash, and how old is the puppy? We enjoyed this sunrise chat and moved on. I left that corner of the road feeling a little more connected to my surroundings and happy that Lily had had a chance to meet another face in our neighborhood.

When Gregory was in kindergarten, he used to enjoy talking about sports to a couple of dads who were regularly at the playground. I didn't know these dads, but Greg started building a relationship with them around a common interest. I loved watching this little five-year-old boy communicate with these men like he was one of the guys. I like that he trusted the world enough to strike up an impromptu conversation. I didn't direct him or even engage, it was just a joy to watch. I always want him to have that feeling, to understand that people everywhere are waiting to make a connection and share a little bit of themselves.

iRule Tip: Let them be bored! Technology use does not need to be the default activity when there is a pause in life. Boredom is a time for creativity, silliness, and imagination—in children, teens, and adults. Make a family list of or guide to the benefits of being bored (or unplugged). What are some things you can do? And ask the reverse question: "What happens if we are never bored and always engaged? What experiences do we lose?"

iRule: Mess Up! Make Mistakes! It's Okay to Be Human!

> **My iRule:** You will mess up. I will take away your phone. We will sit down and talk about it. We will start over again. You and I, we are always learning. I am on your team. We are in this together.

This is parenting. This contract rule can apply to any number of parenting situations in children, from two-year-olds in toilet training to our adult children. This goes beyond the borders of technology and defines what it really means to be an engaged, present parent.

The biggest question I am asked about the contract is if it is working. And while it is working for my Greg at this point, I truly believe that mistakes will happen. He will violate my trust or push the boundaries at some point, especially when the newness and excitement of the gift have worn off. And I hope I catch him! I hope I am right there with him, enforcing the consequences and helping him learn and grow. One year into his iPhone ownership and iRules contract, Greg has totally flourished. He has respected our agreement.

A teacher thanked me for bringing the original iRules contract to the world. She felt that parents were trying to do one of two things: be perfect parents or be pleasing parents. She said she felt that this contract was a reminder to be grounded, to be real and not aspire to be either. She said she was sharing it with parents of her students and e-mailing it to other teachers with the intention of empowering parents to use it as a guide and a reminder in parenthood.

This contract point also applies to other household rules, especially as Greg grows and changes. I do not want a perfect child. I want a child that can come to me in his darkest moment without shame, knowing that I love him unconditionally. I want him to know that I, his mother, am his biggest and greatest advocate. I will hold high expectations for him, because I believe in his gifts, but I will always be there to help build him up again when he stumbles. There is nothing we cannot get through together.

There are times when I hear stories about a child making a choice that's a mistake, or getting caught up in a situation online and waiting too long to turn to a trusted adult. They were embarrassed or scared or lost and confused and did nothing instead. They suffered unnecessarily. They wanted it to go away. They thought they could fix it. Please, parents, make sure your children know they can come to you no matter the circumstance. Do not allow them to face the technology alone. Say it to them, again and again. Be direct: *There is nothing you can do online or in life that I will not help you get through. I might not like it, there might be consequences, but I will always be here for you. Do not ever feel alone. I mean it.*

I have asked parent after parent, "What must your child know about technology?" And sure, there are plenty of answers, like "If you wouldn't want your mother [or grandmother or little sister] to read it, don't write it," and "Know that you can't take back what you post. It's permanent," and "Respect yourself." But more importantly, and almost universally, I hear over and over again, "Talk to us. Come to us. We are here for you no matter what. We will help you. We will guide you. Our love is unconditional. There's nothing we can't get through together." Know that this is an intangible piece of your family iRules.

My Viral iRules

When I decided to share Greg's iRules contract publicly, the response was electric. We were up to our eyeballs in global interviews, media requests, e-mails, and discussions. Greg and I had a blast together,

Living with iRules
An Interview the Hofmann Fab Five

Gregory: I think the original iRules that you gave to me were things I would do already. You probably didn't even need to write them down. But it was also a reminder that I'm not left alone to handle the technology. The rules aren't hard to follow because we agreed on them. They represent our family, they aren't forced on me like a tyrant [would do]. I wouldn't change anything, except it would be nice to have it at school if I have a change of plans midway through the day; I could just call you instead of going to the office to call. But even that's not a big deal. Honestly, Mom, it's just all about respect. Me, you, and Dad respecting each other, me and my friends respecting each other, it's not that complicated or even a big deal.

Brendan: It's not hard to follow our family iRules. The games I can't play are rated M for seventeen-year-olds and since I'm eleven I know I can't play them anyway. Plus I have even better games like *Minecraft*, *NBA [Live]*, *Madden [NFL]*, and *FIFA*. Daddy says a lot of those games [rated M] aren't good for me, so I just listen to him. I know I can't text or use social networks on my iPod. Sometimes that stinks because everyone is talking about it.

spending all this time and energy showing the world a slice of our full life. His buddies rooted for him, his teachers praised him, his basketball team called him "Hollywood." Weeks into the chaos, he turned to me and said, "I still don't know what the big deal is. Is anyone going to ask

What are some of our family's iRules?

Ella, Lily, and Cassidy

- No games on school days, only on weekends.
- No sneaking the iPad or Brendan's iPod or Mom's or Dad's or Greg's phone.
- Do not do the games for too long because they will rot your brain or make you sick.
- Do not touch Mom's computer while she's writing a book.
- Keep Mom's iPad books right where the bookmark was. Don't make it go from Chapter 7 to Chapter 9 by clicking the corner again and again.
- Only use games and songs and videos Mom and Dad know about. Lots of stuff is inappropriate for kids—like gross or mean or boring or blood splattering.
- Never text and drive. Even Mommy can't. She has to ask us to text things for her, like "Auntie Kiki, bring us over some food." And we can only text from her phone when she tells us to because she can scroll it later and find out.
- Don't watch TV and play [with] the iPad at the same time.
- Ask Mom and Dad if you want to get a new game. Brendan types in the password.
- Don't get addicted.

us something new? I think I'm all done with this." And like that, we split ways. I carried the broader discussion on parenting, technology, and respect on to larger platforms. He returned the contract to its original purpose in our home.

When I created the iRules contract, I did not anticipate having to defend it or having it held up as genius. Like my boy said in an interview, "This contract is so my mom." I was bombarded with criticism: "Controlling!" "Bossy!" "Outdated!" I was overwhelmed with praise: "Beautiful!" "Funny!" "Modern!" And more than ever, I had to be so certain of myself, so confident in my own truth that I stood by it without being dependent on others' acceptance or contempt. I'm tougher than I was because of our viral iRules contract. My head is clearer. My voice, more certain. I was unexpectedly asked to stand up for my family, to model a belief system of integrity and authenticity to a global audience.

Late at night when my iRules contract first exploded, I'd lie wide awake, buzzing with media overload. Why did this matter so much? What was this intense buildup of energy underneath the contract? Was I crazy for putting myself and my family out there so publicly? As days turned into weeks and weeks into months, I saw it. Active parenting is vital, being engaged with our families is crucial. Teaching self-respect and consideration of one another and nurturing real human connection in our homes and communities are paramount. Then, deeper still, trusting ourselves to know what is best for our own families—even if it doesn't look the same—is empowering.

For me, the contract craze became a rallying cry for all parents to believe in themselves, to seek answers, to crawl out from under the pressure of perfection, to embody their humanness, to risk being fools by taking action, to fully participate in the name of raising whole people. It became a message and a movement in my heart. Born from love for our children, we find the courage to hold each other up as we navigate what is new, what is unknown, what is real. It is our obligation as parents to rise to the challenge as we blaze this new trail of technology with our families.

So go ahead, mess it up. Seriously. Start a dialogue with your children, make an iRules contract, fumble. Be uncomfortable talking about porn or nudies or cyberbullying. Let it be awkward. Learn to use social networking sites, get accounts, follow and friend your kid. Let him roll his eyes at you. Stand up against language you don't like, selfies that make you squirm, media that make you mad. Know your family. Put your damn devices away, even if it's hard work and your e-mails go unanswered and your daughter doesn't speak to you. Eventually she will. That is the whole point. Let siblings fight, let it be too loud, too messy, too much. Bask in the imperfections of raising a family. Hold your babies and big kids by the hand and by the heart. Imprint all that is sacred to you at the center of their beings. Read to them. Dance with them. Play. Go to the park, sit down at the table for a meal, take a ride in the car, look into each other's eyeballs. Connect. Talk to other parents. Build a village. Pay attention. Listen. Make your contract your own. Let it slide sometimes. But be firm when you feel that parenting pull. Fuel them with resiliency. Grow them on gratitude. Teach them to sweat. Offer your forgiveness. Trust your instincts. Trust your kid. Show up. Every single day, show up. Some days there will be fire in your eyes, some days there will be tears. But most days there will be joy if you just pause long enough to let it in. The only way to get it wrong is to believe that you are just parenting the technology. No, people, you are parenting. Do not hide—step out, step up, and raise your family. You are the only one that knows how.

The Workbook

U se this final section as a tool kit to take the iRules concept out of this book and into your home. This practical guide can serve as a reference as the technology and your children change and grow. Additionally, I have created a glossary that will define popular tech terms and suggest some Web sites for you to use.

The Core Principles

Respect

Be kind to others, tell the truth, use your voice for good, create positive relationships, eat well, sleep well, love yourself, be brave, lead.

Responsibility

Say "please" and "thank you," make eye contact, work hard, value what you have, bask in gratitude, honor your family, set high standards, engage, exercise, think.

Live Fully

Have fun, play, go outside, be silly, be willing to make mistakes, create, imagine, be curious, seek, serve, give back.

The Core Components

iRules: A living and breathing contract for behavior related to the use of technology. Its components must suit your home, your parenting style, and your needs. Every family has to write its own iRules, a set of agreements that are appropriate for their children's ages and the types of technology they use.

Slow Tech Parenting: A philosophy about conscious living and authenticity in technology use and family values. Slow Tech Parenting fosters real, personal connections and interactions in our everyday experiences rather than allowing technology to dominate the family's habits and lifestyle.

Tech Talk: A deliberate conversation you must have with each of your children regarding the specific technology they use.

I Want iRules— A Recipe for Tech Success

○ Assess the technology in your home. What technologies are your children using?

○ What is your relationship with technology—beginner, advanced, addicted? Do you understand how to use all of the technology that your children do?

○ List the accounts that you know they have—video games, Instagram, Twitter, Facebook, Snapchat, Web site memberships, e-mail, iChat. If you don't know or aren't sure, ask!

○ Do they have passwords on any of these accounts? Do you want to know them?

○ When do they use or play with each tech device?

○ How do they act when they are engaged in using technology?

○ Do you notice more of a behavior change with certain types of technology use than others?

O Are they secretive or have you had problems with their use of any technology?

O Do you have any rules or agreements already? Do you enforce them? Are they working?

O What is important or of interest to your family besides technology—academics, sports or extracurricular activities, outdoor play, healthy eating, pleasure reading, music?

O Does the technology interfere with or negatively affect school-work, household chores, or other commitments? Where does it fall on the child's list of priorities?

O Identify when tech use is not allowed, such as during meals, while at church, during visits with relatives, in public, during friends' visits, at school, while driving.

O Who pays for the technology? Who is responsible for the device if it gets damaged?

O Is there a tech curfew or time limit on the use of certain tech-nologies? Is it enforced?

O When is the technology to be left behind or shut off? Do you want to enforce digital-free days or times?

O Identify your thoughts on and beliefs about video game ratings and age-appropriate tech activities.

O What are your fears about technology? Do you know how to use parental controls and teach your children privacy settings?

Explore these concepts with your spouse or partner and any other adult that has an active and vested interest in raising your children. Come to an agreement together on the ideal tech guidelines for your family both inside and outside of the home. Bring your children into the discussion deliberately and with purpose. Open the dialogue. Ask questions and let them ask you questions. Discuss the things you love and how they fit into your life. Ask them how important technology is to them. Introduce the idea of drawing up house iRules. Express that you want to protect and respect them. Tell them these rules are created in love and trust, but it is your primary responsibility, like any-thing else, to teach them to behave with technology. Compile a set of age-appropriate iRules for each child since ages, personalities, and needs may vary. Set consequences if the rules are violated.

Consider iRules for yourself: Is your work following you home? Are social networking sites getting all of your attention? Are constant text conversations distracting you? Consider your own tech etiquette a model for your family. Keep the iRules alive! Refer to them often. Discuss what's working and what isn't. Tell your friends and neighbors about your house iRules so they will be applied consistently no matter where your children are. Continue to reassess them as your children grow and change and as the technology changes. Be proud! Active parenting is hard work!

Before Your Tech Talk

O **Come Together!** A key component in making your iRules a suc-cess is to have complete accord with everyone who is parenting your children with you. This is crucial and cannot be avoided. Teamwork makes the dream work!

O **Are You Mad?** Assess your own feelings about and values related to specific technologies. Note these feelings so you can address specific boundaries head-on while being aware of your emotional temperature in each instance.

O **Name Them, Then Tame Them!** Does the technology in your home scare you? What are you afraid of? List it!

O **Kid Profile:** Think about your child. List their age, interests, tendencies, personality traits, struggles, etc. This will help you brainstorm what needs to be addressed by your iRules.

Ready to Tech Talk?

Have an in-person meeting with your child—eyeballs to eyeballs—with all electronic devices (yours and theirs!) locked away.

Tech Talk Phase 1: Info Gathering

O   What technologies are you using?

O   Can you explain the basics and teach me how to use the ones I'm not familiar with?

O   Will you show me your online profile?

O   When do you like to use the technology and why?

Tech Talk Phase 2: Define Expectations

O   For each technology used, present your ideal vision for appropriate use, including time limits, expectations, etc.

O   Formalize your expectations for family tech use.

O   Open a discussion or arrange a Tech Talk at any time.

O   Be clear and direct, but open enough to ask and answer questions.

Tech Talk Phase 3: Meet Again!

O   Keep the Tech Talks alive! Don't wait until there is a crisis or struggle. Schedule regular Tech Talks to keep the communication open.

O   For example, did your daughter get a new social networking account or a new iPad as she entered high school? Come together again for a Tech Talk.

O   Have you noticed a change in behavior? Perhaps your son is purchasing a series of video games without your approval and it's making you uncertain? Schedule another Tech Talk.

iRule Tip: It is best to meet with each child individually for a Tech Talk. But you may have some house iRules that apply to everyone. Feel free to meet as a group when discussing iRules that apply to the whole family.

Assess Maturity before Each Technology Purchase

Sample questions to ask yourself:

- ○ Are household chores being done?
- ○ Are grades up to our family's standards?
- ○ Are responsibilities being met?
- ○ Do we currently struggle over technology, apps, sites, etc., before I allow something new?
- ○ Will this new technology bring our household more struggle than joy?
- ○ Am I doing this just because all of my child's peers have it?
- ○ How will my child use this technology? Is having it a necessity or a privilege?

Work

What rules and ideals do you have for valuing material possessions? How do your children contribute to the family system and daily operations of your household? Outline your expectations for your children's contributions to the technology based on your beliefs. Assess the value of the technology in your home and consider the contribution your child makes to support that value. Below is a simple exercise to see if your household's balancing of technology and work fits your needs and expectations.

Tech Privileges

Child's financial contribution to technology: _____

_____

Child's extracurricular activities: _____

Child's financial contribution to activities: _____

_____

Family system contribution: _____

Financial payment for family system contribution: _____

Assessment of balance: _____

Passwords

Knowing the passwords on technology accounts is a clear opportunity to provide protection in an often unpoliced world of social networking and online activities.

○ List all of the online accounts your child has.

○ Do you have the passwords to these accounts?

○ Do you understand how to navigate and operate each account and activity in the event that you needed to access it? If not, learn to use the technology that your children use. Be present in these places. If your child is on Twitter, get a Twitter account. Follow each other.

○ Have a presence in the technology just like you have a presence away from the technology.

Manners and Etiquette

○ Make a list of your expectations for your children in their everyday lives in relation to how they treat others. Then apply those same expectations to the technology that they use.

○ Make a list of tech behaviors you have observed outside the family that bother you.

○ Ask your child if they've seen the same behaviors. Do they have any to add?

○ Adapt your iRules to make sure that your child doesn't violate your family's manners and etiquette values.

School

Ask these questions before providing your children with access to technology. These are all important questions to ask when deciding whether to allow at-home technology to go to school.

- ○ Is my child a good student?
- ○ How will having a portable electronic device in school help or enhance the experience?
- ○ Is my child easily distracted by the devices?
- ○ What is the school's policy?

Say This about Selfies!

- ○ I want to see your eyes.
- ○ I want to see your face.
- ○ I want to see your smile.
- ○ I want to see the parts of you that are whole.
- ○ I do not want to see inappropriate portions or sections of you.
- ○ Every picture you post of yourself must include your face—that is the real you!

I Found a Nudie Pic—HELP!

Depending on whether your child is the sender or receiver, be prepared to ask some version of these questions.

- ○ Why do you have this picture?
- ○ Why did you send this picture?
- ○ Do you have permission to have this picture?
- ○ Was it sent directly to you by the person in the picture?
- ○ Have you forwarded or shared this picture with anyone else?
- ○ Were you pressured to send this picture?

Call a meeting with your child.

- ○ Create a space of trust, safety, and privacy.
- ○ Ask the above questions. Get the story.

○ If what you learn indicates that this is a case of abuse or misuse, take immediate action: Take the phone or device away, inform law enforcement officials if necessary (when it involves minors communicating with adults, strangers, force or coercion, bribery, cyberbullying), and if you feel overwhelmed, seek professional advice and guidance.

○ If you learn that the matter involves consenting peers, assess what needs to be done. Depending on the exact circumstances, you might delete the pictures, ask for or make an apology, have a conversation with the other child's family, and/or discuss the risks and consequences with your child.

How We Stay Present

○ We schedule regular stretches of free time away from technology.

○ We talk. A lot.

○ We hold each other accountable.

○ We designate no-fuss tech time for free play using technology.

○ We designate times when phones are to be turned off or set to silent or DO NOT DISTURB.

○ We love many things. This helps us to stay alive and engaged.

Tools to Prevent Fear of Missing Out

○ Gratitude is contagious. Be thankful for it all.

○ Keep a daily or weekly gratitude journal.

○ Religiously praise the people around you.

○ Tell your kids how awesome your home is.

○ Praise your community, schools, region.

○ Go outside.

○ Set goals.

Glossary

Here you'll find a clear, user-friendly glossary of popular terms, sites, and apps mentioned in the book.

app: a computer program for mobile devices that performs a particular function

creeper: someone who views your online profile multiple times, frequently commenting, trolling, and getting involved in a, well, creepy way; also called a lurker or stalker

direct message: a personal message sent from one user to another and not viewable by other users on a social networking site; also called a private message

e-tox: a period of time when technology use is purposely avoided; also known as a digital diet

Facebook: a social networking site where each user has a designated page for communicating with other users who have been accepted as friends

Facebook wall: a page in a Facebook user's profile that shows their own posts as well as those of users approved as friends

friend fail: unkind or unfair treatment via electronic means by a friend having the same level of social power

hashtag: a word or phrase prefaced with a # in a tweet that signifies a trend or popular topic; clicking on the hashtag returns all the other posts and pictures on Twitter that have used a hashtag including that word or phrase

Instagram: a social networking site used for sharing pictures and videos that includes tools for editing, enhancing, and commenting on the images and offers users the option of designating their accounts viewable by anyone or only by approved users

Kik Messenger: a texting app for smartphones and iPods

like: a button on a Facebook page that a user clicks to indicate approval of material posted by others

notification: a message sent to a social networking user that they have received a new post

nudie: a naked or topless picture shared or received usually through text messaging or a social networking site

online gaming: playing computer games with people in different locations through an Internet connection; usually allows all players to hear each other

parent creeper: a parent that monitors their own and others' children online to learn what teens are discussing

Permission to Post!: the subject's approval to tag, post, or share a picture of someone

profile pic: a picture associated with a particular user's profile on a social networking account

retweet: a post on Twitter that is a forwarded to another user

screenshot: a photograph taken of what appears on the screen of the mobile device or tablet used to take the picture

selfie: a self-portrait typically taken with a camera phone and then posted and shared on social networking sites

sexting: the sending and receiving of text messages, online conversations, or pictures containing sexual material

Snapchat: a picture-sharing social networking site on which an image sent to another user self-destructs seconds after it is viewed; often referred to as "the sexting app" because some account holders use it for that purpose, assuming no record of the photo will remain

status update: a new post made by a user to their Facebook page

subtweet: a subliminal tweet that directly refers to a person without naming them

trolling: Internet users who deliberately cause trouble online through emotional or provoking comments and conversations

tweet: a post of 140 characters or less on Twitter

Twitter: a social networking site on which users post messages of 140 characters or less; a user's page can be designated as private to permit only approved followers to view the user's tweets

Vine: a Twitter feature that allows users to post and share six seconds or less of looping video

Xbox Kinect: a piece of hardware for the Xbox game console that tracks the user's movements and responds to voice commands; also includes a camera that can be used for taking pictures and for video chats

Popular Social Networking Sites for Tweens and Teens 2013/2014

Facebook

Twitter

Vine

Instagram

Snapchat

FaceTime

Kik Messenger

Ask.fm

Xbox Live

Popular Abbreviations for Online Communication

asl: age, sex, location

bff: best friends forever

brb: be right back

hbu: how 'bout you

hmu: hit me up

idc: I don't care

idk: I don't know

ily(2): I love you (too)

irl: in real life

lol: laugh/laughing out loud

oh: overheard

omg: oh my God/goodness

omw: on my way

paw: parents are watching

rolf: rolling on the floor laughing

rt: retweet

stfu: shut the F up

tia: thanks in advance

tmi: too much information

wtf: what the F

Acknowledgments

Speaking, writing, and building a platform about raising children with technology manifested from the deepest parts of my parenting beliefs and philosophies. This was not always easy for me to understand. I do not know why I was called upon, actually thrust into this work. The iPhone contract I created for Gregory was a spiritual gift. When I gathered those thoughts and words together and shared them, something divine occurred from such an ordinary act. I still don't know all the answers, but I'm pretty sure it has to do with speaking from my heart. I am actually relieved to compile this monster list of people to thank because I have been carrying them with me every step of the way during the creation of this book. I want them out, visible on these pages, so you know how vital they were and are to the birth and existence of iRules. And the existence of me.

To My Professional Village

To my *Huffington Post* Parents editor, Farah Miller, for giving my writing millions of eyeballs and giving the iPhone contract wings. To Ben Johnson from *Marketplace Tech* for giving me a regular spot and always making me feel like I was talking to an old friend. To Fauzie and everyone at FSB Associates for your dedication to this project. To Shawna Butler for your trusted guidance. To writing professionals, female powerhouses, and movement leaders like Lenore Skenazy and Rachel Simmons, thank you for always taking the time to say in one way or another, "You can do this." To my publishing house, Rodale, the sales and marketing team, and all the dedicated professionals that worked on bringing this book to life, namely, Yelena Nesbit, Nancy Bailey, and Christopher De Marchis, thank you. Thank you to my brilliant editor, Jennifer Levesque, who said to me during our initial meeting, "You are every woman" and made my heart soar. To Dunlow, Carson and Lerner Literary Agency and the world's most magnificent literary agent, Amy Hughes, thank you. Amy, thank you for seeing what I could not. You are the maker of dreams and I will always be humbled by your gifts. To the zillions of people that read the iPhone contract, thank you.

To My Personal Village

Leslie Santos, thank you for your edits and reads, time and insights right from the start. For having the wisdom to look into my eyes on a rainy March night during the conception of iRules and say, "It needs more you. It needs more of Janell. That's what we all want." To the Sandwich Recreation Department—Guy and Jan—for giving me a professional home while I gathered my forces and giving me the space to fly. To my Oakcrest Cove staff, especially Tricia and Colleen, thank you for being all things while I straddled two worlds. To the counselors, thanks for all of your "field research" and for being so willing to offer up your tech stories to your boss who planned to publish them in her book. You are a special kind of people. To Kellie's peeps that gave me stories and trusted me with slices of their lives. To all of the young people that gave me stories and shared their heartfelt opinions about growing up with technology, you already know the answers; just listen to yourselves. To the educators that we hardly thank enough, thank you for sharing pieces of your professional journeys with technology. To Scott MacDonald, chief of police in Orleans, Massachusetts, for your expertise. To Alicia Mathewson and Andrea Spacek and our powerful, spiritual Trifecta. To Sounding Still Wellness for Rising Star Energy Healings. To Lindsey Mae Photography. To Jas and Erica from Insite Creative for my beautiful Web site. To the people that run and sweat and move with me, you are my tribe . To any one of the million or so yoga classes I dropped into and bowed and opened and let the warrior within reveal herself, thank you. To the places in town where I drink coffee and eat yummy food, the Coffee Roost, Momo's, Café Riverview, Café Chew, you spark my words to life. To the brilliant and beautiful women of Cape Cod and families across the world that shared stories, questions, concerns, ideas, and contributed to this book, thank you. To the "Sandwich Moms" for being the heart of our village every day. To the Sandwich Public Library for being awesome since the very first day I stepped inside. To Dawn and Mary for opening your homes and hearts to Cassidy. To my Canterbury Crew—Susan, Monika, Kathy, Katherine, Betsy—your children are my children, thank you for letting me lean as needed. To Sally, for your guidance and friendship. To the Jordans for always being a bold example of the power of family. To Made By Survivors for saying, "Girl, you can write," and then giving me my first space to do so. And to the survivors, those at risk, and those enslaved in the modern-day slave trade, you cracked open my heart. Your bright eyes and brave hearts are my guiding light. I hold your courage in the center of my chest every day.

To My Sacred Village

To Karen Diane, you are the realest. You are truly the most special friend on the planet. To Uncle Jerry for your consistent, selfless love and the writer's gene. Nana Mae, Nana Reen, and Papa, for always. To Bob and Karen, being a part of your family is one of my life's most treasured gifts. I love you. Dad, for a lifetime of encouraging a girl with fire in her heart to let it burn bright. To Lindsey and Kellie, my love for you is not measurable, you are my home. To the women that came before, I march with your hand in mine, every day of my life. To Mom, all of this I owe to you. It is my honor to be your daughter. To Gregory, Brendan, Ella, Lily, and Cassidy, you are my teachers. Not even love can hold what I feel for you. I am here, on this earth, only to be with you. You are my destiny. To Adam, there are no words. I can only give you the contents of my heart and every minute of my life. You are my holy ground.

Sources

Campaign for a Commercial-Free Childhood. "Help Us Stop the Deceptive Advertising of Baby Apps." http://www.commercialfreechildhood.org/action/help-us-stop-deceptive-advertising-baby-apps

Campaign for a Commercial-Free Childhood. "Laps, Not Apps: One Down, One to Go." *Campaign for a Commercial-Free Childhood Newsletter,* August 2013. http://www.commercialfreechildhood.org/newsletter/august-2013

Centers for Disease Control and Prevention. "Distracted Driving." http://www.cdc.gov/Motorvehiclesafety/Distracted_Driving

DoSomething.org. "11 Facts About Cyberbullying." n.d. http://www.dosomething.org/tipsandtools/11-facts-about-cyber-bullying

Englander, E.. Reducing Bullying and Cyberbullying. Massachusetts Aggression Reduction Center, Bridgewater State University, Bridgewater, MA. http://www.eschoolnews.com/2010/09/24/reducing-bullyingand-cyberbullying/

Entertainment Software Rating Board. "ESRB Ratings Guide." n.d. http://www.esrb.org/ratings/ratings_guide.jsp

Fujita, A., and Ng, C. "Mom Has Son Sign 18-Point Agreement for iPhone." ABCNews.com, December 30, 2012. http://abcnews.go.com/US/massachusetts-mom-son-sign-18-point-agreement-iphone/story?id=18094401

Gutnick, A.L., Robb, M., Takeuchi, L., and Kotler, J. *Always Connected: The New Digital Media Habits of Young Children*. New York: Joan Ganz Cooney Center at Sesame Workshop, March 10, 2011. http://www.joanganzcooneycenter.org/wp-content/uploads/2011/03/jgcc_alwaysconnected.pdf

MacDonald, S. Personal interview, August 10, 2013.

Murphy Kelly, Samantha. "Most Parents Monitor Kids on Facebook—And Have Their Passwords." Mashable.com, January 13, 2012. http://mashable.com/2012/01/13/parents-monitoring-facebook

National Crime Prevention Council. "What Is Cyberbullying?" n.d. http://www.ncpc.org/topics/cyberbullying/what-is-cyberbullying

National Sleep Foundation. "Annual Sleep in America Poll Exploring Connections with Communications Technology Use and Sleep." March 7, 2011. [news release] http://www.sleepfoundation.org/article/press-release/annual-sleep-america-poll-exploring-connections-communications-technology-use-

Post Senning, C., and Post, P. *Teen Manners: From Malls to Meals to Messaging and Beyond*. New York: Collins, 2007.

Post Senning, D. *Emily Post's Manners in a Digital World: Living Well Online*. New York: Open Road, 2013.

Skenazy, L. Personal interview, October 11, 2013.

StopCyberbullying.org. "What Is Cyberbullying, Exactly?" n.d. http://stopcyberbullying. org/what_is_cyberbullying_exactly.html

Strasburger, V.C. "American Academy of Pediatrics Policy Statement: Media Education." *Pediatrics* 126(5):1012–1017, 2010. http://pediatrics.aappublications.org/content/126/5/ 1012.full

Index

softened expectations on, 73–74
teaching, 239
Maturity assessment, for evaluating technology readiness, <u>21</u>, 174, 238
Meaningful family moments, identifying, 217
Meetings, for Tech Talks, 11–12, 237
Messing up, 226–27, 230–31
Money, children's concept of, 108–10
Music
downloads, iRule on, <u>197</u>
technology providing access to, 199–202, <u>200–201</u>

N

Non-tech house rules, <u>88–89</u>
Nudie pictures, <u>149</u>, 240–41

O

Observations, about technology use, 91–95
Online addiction, 187–88
Online behavior, inappropriate discussions about, 32
monitors of, 33–34
when to tell other parents about, 63–64
Online communication, abbreviations for, 246
Online conversations, how to stop, 29–30, 54
Online culture, for girls, 184–85
Online personal games and quizzes, 192–94
Online personalities, 66, 182–84
Online posts
peer rules about, 188–89
typical female, 184, 185

Online profiles, as reflection of children's lives, 65

P

Parental permission, accounts set up without, 13–14
Parental settings, xv, 136, <u>136</u>
Parental tech presence, children's desire for, <u>29</u>
Parents
of children's friends
conversations with, 45, 209–10
importance of meeting, 84
as creepers, 31–32
guiding children's online world, 195, 227
as iRule creators, xix
iRules contract empowering, 226, 230–31
manners toward, 81–82
partnering with, 66–67
pornography discussions among, 130–32
quiz for, xxv–xxvi
reporting concerning behaviors to, 63–64
technology limits for, <u>211</u>, <u>221</u>, 222–23, 236
technology overuse by, 18–20, 236
technology overwhelming, xvii–xviii, 5
texting children in school, 116
of trailblazing generation, 179
in two households, consistent iRules and, 210, <u>211</u>, 212
Password logbook, 26
Password privacy, attitudes about, 32–33
Passwords
parental knowledge of, 22–23, 25–26, 30, 33, 37, 234, 239
prohibited sharing of, 37–38